Culture Wars

OPPOSING VIEWPOINTS ®

Mary E. Williams, *Book Editor*

Daniel Leone, *President*
Bonnie Szumski, *Publisher*
Scott Barbour, *Managing Editor*
Helen Cothran, *Senior Editor*

OPPOSING
VIEWPOINTS®
SERIES

GREENHAVEN
PRESS®

THOMSON
—————
GALE

San Diego • Detroit • New York • San Francisco • Cleveland
New Haven, Conn. • Waterville, Maine • London • Munich

LIBRARY OF CONGRESS CATALOGING-IN-PUBLICATION DATA

Culture wars : opposing viewpoints / Mary E. Williams, book editor.
    p. cm. — (Opposing viewpoints series)
    Includes bibliographical references and index.
    ISBN 0-7377-1679-7 (lib. bdg. : alk. paper) —
    ISBN 0-7377-1680-0 (pbk. : alk. paper)
      1. United States—Social conditions—1980– . 2. Popular culture—United States. 3. Social problems—United States. 4. United States—Social life and customs. 5. United States—Politics and government—1989– . I. Williams, Mary E., 1960– . II. Opposing viewpoints series (Unnumbered)
    HN59.2 .C85 2003
    306'.0973—dc21
                                                                    2002042611

Printed in the United States of America

"Congress shall make no law... abridging the freedom of speech, or of the press."

First Amendment to the U.S. Constitution

The basic foundation of our democracy is the First Amendment guarantee of freedom of expression. The Opposing Viewpoints Series is dedicated to the concept of this basic freedom and the idea that it is more important to practice it than to enshrine it.

Contents

Why Consider Opposing Viewpoints?

"The only way in which a human being can make some approach to knowing the whole of a subject is by hearing what can be said about it by persons of every variety of opinion and studying all modes in which it can be looked at by every character of mind. No wise man ever acquired his wisdom in any mode but this."

John Stuart Mill

In our media-intensive culture it is not difficult to find differing opinions. Thousands of newspapers and magazines and dozens of radio and television talk shows resound with differing points of view. The difficulty lies in deciding which opinion to agree with and which "experts" seem the most credible. The more inundated we become with differing opinions and claims, the more essential it is to hone critical reading and thinking skills to evaluate these ideas. Opposing Viewpoints books address this problem directly by presenting stimulating debates that can be used to enhance and teach these skills. The varied opinions contained in each book examine many different aspects of a single issue. While examining these conveniently edited opposing views, readers can develop critical thinking skills such as the ability to compare and contrast authors' credibility, facts, argumentation styles, use of persuasive techniques, and other stylistic tools. In short, the Opposing Viewpoints Series is an ideal way to attain the higher-level thinking and reading skills so essential in a culture of diverse and contradictory opinions.

In addition to providing a tool for critical thinking, Opposing Viewpoints books challenge readers to question their own strongly held opinions and assumptions. Most people form their opinions on the basis of upbringing, peer pressure, and personal, cultural, or professional bias. By reading carefully balanced opposing views, readers must directly confront new ideas as well as the opinions of those with whom they disagree. This is not to simplistically argue that everyone who reads opposing views will—or should—change his or her opinion. Instead, the series enhances readers' understanding of their own views by encouraging confrontation with opposing ideas. Careful examination of others' views can lead to the readers' understanding of the logical inconsistencies in their own opinions, perspective on why they hold an opinion, and the consideration of the possibility that their opinion requires further evaluation.

Evaluating Other Opinions

To ensure that this type of examination occurs, Opposing Viewpoints books present all types of opinions. Prominent spokespeople on different sides of each issue as well as well-known professionals from many disciplines challenge the reader. An additional goal of the series is to provide a forum for other, less known, or even unpopular viewpoints. The opinion of an ordinary person who has had to make the decision to cut off life support from a terminally ill relative, for example, may be just as valuable and provide just as much insight as a medical ethicist's professional opinion. The editors have two additional purposes in including these less known views. One, the editors encourage readers to respect others' opinions—even when not enhanced by professional credibility. It is only by reading or listening to and objectively evaluating others' ideas that one can determine whether they are worthy of consideration. Two, the inclusion of such viewpoints encourages the important critical thinking skill of objectively evaluating an author's credentials and bias. This evaluation will illuminate an author's reasons for taking a particular stance on an issue and will aid in readers' evaluation of the author's ideas.

It is our hope that these books will give readers a deeper understanding of the issues debated and an appreciation of the complexity of even seemingly simple issues when good and honest people disagree. This awareness is particularly important in a democratic society such as ours in which people enter into public debate to determine the common good. Those with whom one disagrees should not be regarded as enemies but rather as people whose views deserve careful examination and may shed light on one's own.

Thomas Jefferson once said that "difference of opinion leads to inquiry, and inquiry to truth." Jefferson, a broadly educated man, argued that "if a nation expects to be ignorant and free . . . it expects what never was and never will be." As individuals and as a nation, it is imperative that we consider the opinions of others and examine them with skill and discernment. The Opposing Viewpoints Series is intended to help readers achieve this goal.

David L. Bender and Bruno Leone,
Founders

Greenhaven Press anthologies primarily consist of previously published material taken from a variety of sources, including periodicals, books, scholarly journals, newspapers, government documents, and position papers from private and public organizations. These original sources are often edited for length and to ensure their accessibility for a young adult audience. The anthology editors also change the original titles of these works in order to clearly present the main thesis of each viewpoint and to explicitly indicate the opinion presented in the viewpoint. These alterations are made in consideration of both the reading and comprehension levels of a young adult audience. Every effort is made to ensure that Greenhaven Press accurately reflects the original intent of the authors included in this anthology.

Introduction

"Several of the most contentious and passionate issues in current politics revolve around what can be called 'cultural' issues."

—*Rhys H. Williams*

"Culture wars" became a popular catchphrase during the 1980s and 1990s—especially in 1992 when presidential hopeful Patrick Buchanan delivered his campaign speech to the Republican National Convention. Addressing concerns over such controversial issues as abortion, affirmative action, and arts funding, he proclaimed that conservatives must declare a cultural revolution—"a war for the nation's soul." Buchanan sees this war as a political and moral battle largely between liberal secular forces and conservative religious forces. In a similar vein, sociologist James Davison Hunter, the author of several books on American political and cultural conflict, defines the culture wars as ongoing ideological debates between two opposing camps. Hunter maintains that these debates typically occur between various "orthodox" (conservative or traditional) and "progressive" (liberal or modern) interests, cutting across the realms of politics, religion, ethics, economics, popular culture, and education.

The phrase "culture wars" is derived from the German word *Kulturkampf,* which literally means "a struggle for the control of the culture." In late nineteenth-century Germany, for example, chancellor Otto von Bismarck launched a *Kulturkampf* against the Catholic Church, expelling Jesuits from the country and passing laws that restricted the church's influence in education and politics. Due to strong opposition from German citizens, however, Bismarck was forced to abandon his *Kulturkampf* in 1878.

A significant early battle in America's *Kulturkampf*—in this case, a conflict between traditional religion and modern science—occurred during the famous Scopes "monkey trial" of 1925. John T. Scopes, a science instructor in Tennessee, was found guilty of teaching the Darwinian theory of evolution, which at that time was illegal in his state. Although Scopes was convicted, the Tennessee supreme court eventually overturned the verdict on a technicality. More importantly, the trial was seen as a victory for supporters of science and modernism because literal interpretations of the Bible were soundly challenged on the witness stand. Subsequently, religious fundamentalists' attempts to criminalize the teaching of evolution in other states were largely unsuccessful.

As the twentieth century progressed, politically liberal ideals, which tend to emphasize tolerance, collective responsibility, and the use of government to improve social conditions, became increasingly influential. During the 1960s and 1970s, for example, activists and legislators won several victories for the civil rights and women's rights movements. In 1964, Congress passed a Civil Rights Act that prohibited job discrimination based on age, race, religion, gender, or national origin. This legislation had a tremendous impact on American culture: Racial segregation in public facilities was outlawed, affirmative action policies were implemented, and large numbers of women entered the paid workforce. In addition, mounting concern for the poor led to an expansion of government under the "Great Society" programs started by President Lyndon Johnson. While liberals generally view the 1960s and 1970s as watershed decades, conservatives often contend that the decline in the influence of traditional religious values during those years harmed American culture. They decry the 1962 Supreme Court decision outlawing state-sponsored school prayer, for instance, as well as the 1973 *Roe v. Wade* decision that legalized abortion in the first two trimesters of pregnancy.

The late twentieth century, however, witnessed an upsurge in political conservatism—an ideology that champions traditional values, individual responsibility, and the minimal use of government for social support. In 1980, a broad majority of voters elected conservative Republican Ronald Reagan as president. Reagan openly advocated a more conservative approach to politics and culture by opposing government spending, abortion, and restrictions on school prayer. His leadership changed the tenor of national debate, and right-wing religious organizations, such as the Christian Coalition and the Moral Majority, became politically and culturally influential. For example, as the rates of violent crime, drug use, and divorce rose, a growing number of Americans agreed with the conservative argument that such trends were the result of a decline in traditional family values and an amoral popular culture. Moreover, controversies over morality, free speech, and the definition of acceptable cultural standards began to dominate headlines, the courts, and college campuses.

One such dispute emerged over whether the federal government's National Endowment for the Arts should have funded an exhibition of the work of Robert Mapplethorpe, whose homoerotic photographs offended some viewers. Another controversy arose over whether school curricula should emphasize the intellectual traditions of Western civilization or adopt a multicultural approach to literature and history. Still another nationwide debate involved the question of whether single- or gay-parented families are as effective as traditional two-parent families at raising children.

In 1992, the conservative-versus-liberal split was apparent in the presidential race between incumbent President George H.W. Bush and his Democratic opponent, Bill Clinton. While Bush ran on a platform emphasizing traditional family values and the importance of personal morality, Clinton stressed the need for economic renewal. Many liberals contended that the disturbing social trends of the previous years had been fueled by the economic recession that occurred during Bush's presidency. They believed the economic strategy of the Reagan and Bush administrations had exacerbated poverty and placed financial pressures on workers and families—factors which they felt had likely contributed to the increasing crime and divorce rates.

The economy flourished during Clinton's presidency, and by the mid-1990s some analysts noted that the rates of violent crime and teen pregnancy were actually decreasing. Nevertheless, many conservatives still feared that America was facing serious cultural decline. "Unless the exploding social pathologies of the past thirty years are reversed," warned conservative analyst William Bennett, "they will lead to the decline and perhaps even to the fall of the American republic." For a contingent of conservatives, the last few years of Clinton's presidency seemed to bear this warning out.

In 1998, Clinton was impeached on charges that he had lied under oath and obstructed justice in an attempt to conceal an affair he had had with White House intern Monica Lewinsky. Although the Senate acquitted Clinton in 1999, his actions sparked a national debate about how a politician's personal moral standards might affect his or her leadership. Polls taken during the scandal revealed that most Americans agreed that Clinton did not have high moral standards, but they still largely approved of his job performance and opposed congressional attempts to remove him from office. In fact, a survey conducted during the impeachment placed Clinton's approval rating at 73 percent—the highest of his presidency. Analysts like Paul Weyrich, former president of the conservative Heritage Foundation, maintained that the public's indifference to Clinton's affair was a sign that conservatives had "probably lost the culture war." In a widely publicized 1999 statement, Weyrich claimed that American society was becoming an "ever-wider sewer" and that the country was "caught up in a cultural collapse of historic proportions." Contending that conservatives had failed to implement a political agenda that would protect the country's traditional values, Weyrich advised conservatives to "drop out" of American culture and find nonpolitical ways to preserve genuine morality.

Conservative politicians did not, for the most part, follow Weyrich's advice. In fact, after conservative Republican George W. Bush became president in 2001, many activists redoubled their efforts to promote right-wing agendas in local and national politics. According to liberal commentator Jim Whittle, the White House has "a close alliance with the religious right in the nation's war over values." But whether America's *Kulturkampf* can ultimately be "won" remains to be seen. History suggests that conservative and progressive ideologies will each continue to challenge and influence the other, with neither side gaining total victory. This is perhaps a sign of a healthy and vibrant democracy. *Culture Wars: Opposing Viewpoints* offers readers a spectrum of opinion on the national *Kulturkampf* in the following chapters: What Is the State of America's Culture Wars? Is American Culture in Decline? What Political and Cultural Influences Benefit Society? Should Government Regulate Cultural Values? Analyzing the responses to these questions will give readers a broad contemporary overview of America's culturally driven debates.

CHAPTER 1

What Is the State of America's Culture Wars?

Chapter Preface

In his often-quoted 1994 book, *Before the Shooting Begins: Searching for Democracy in America's Culture War*, sociologist James Davison Hunter described the culture wars as ongoing ideological disputes between various "orthodox" and "progressive" interests. Hunter maintained that the continuing liberal-versus-conservative arguments over controversial issues such as abortion, feminism, and homosexuality had become increasingly polarized and hostile—so much so that the nation was suffering from the lack of a more moderate and complex understanding of contemporary social problems. Democratic debate and discussion had become, in Hunter's view, "obnoxious, at the very least; dangerous at the worst."

Not all analysts agree with Hunter. Sociologist Rhys H. Williams, editor of *Culture Wars in American Politics*, grants that there are significant differences in opinion between liberals and conservatives but contends that these conflicts are not as widespread or as polarized as Hunter and other commentators have claimed. America's representative democracy has a moderating effect on society, Williams asserts, and the phrase "culture wars" characterizes the heated rhetoric of politicians and activists rather than an actual rift in the population at large. In Williams's opinion, "Apathy is the dominant feature of public opinion. That's why activists feel compelled to pitch their appeals in strident terms."

Recent events suggest that both Hunter and Williams are partly correct: America's culture wars are hostile and divisive, but at the same time, their magnitude has been exaggerated. Commentators' reactions to the terrorist attacks of September 11, 2001, for example, revealed deep—and often bitter—differences of opinion between liberals and conservatives. Many prominent liberal analysts opposed military responses to the attacks and argued that Americans needed to examine the causes of terrorism, which they believed were partly based on a justified anger about U.S. support for repressive political regimes around the world. *Nation* columnist Katha Pollitt stated that she would not allow her daughter to fly the American flag because it "stands for jingoism and vengeance and war." In turn, many conservatives, who largely supported military retaliation for the attacks, argued that liberal critics were being characteristically unpatriotic and were blaming the United States for terrorism against its own people. Conservative author Paul Hollander wrote that for liberals, "American society is deeply flawed and uniquely repellent—unjust, corrupt, destructive, soulless, inhumane, inauthentic and incapable of satisfying basic, self-evident human needs." Progressives countered that liberal criticisms of government policy were taken out of context and misrepresented as hatred of America.

Liberals were not the only ones criticized for their opinions on the September 11 attacks. When Christian fundamentalists Jerry Falwell and Pat Robertson claimed that the attacks were God's judgment on an America that tolerates abortionists, feminists, homosexuals, and civil libertarians, their comments were strongly denounced by both conservatives and liberals. Some liberals, however, argued that Falwell-style fundamentalism was as dangerous as the militant Islamic fundamentalism that had inspired the terrorist attacks. Columnist Ellen Willis, for example, asserted that "the enemy is fundamentalism itself—not [just] the 'evil' anti-American fundamentalists, as opposed to the allegedly friendly kind." Conservatives responded that those who agreed with Willis were harshly and wrongly condemning Christian fundamentalists—most of whom are not violent extremists.

Although analysts' debates about the September 11 attacks were often antagonistic, most Americans share neither Pollitt's disdain for the flag nor Falwell's contempt for liberalism and tolerance. Therefore, Williams's conclusion that the culture wars are more the domain of politicians and pundits than of the public seems valid. However, Hunter's warnings about the polarized nature of culture wars rhetoric should not be taken lightly since Americans rely on politicians to make crucial policy decisions. The public should beware of politicians who resort to hostility, exaggerated claims, and misrepresentations of opponents' views. As *Washington Post* editor Chris Lehmann maintains, "If we really want our culture to bear the sort of meaning we imagine it has, we should try approaching it as the outcome of . . . reasoned debate rather than as a spoil of war."

"A moral majority no longer exists in America. We [conservatives] probably have lost the overall culture war."

The Culture Wars Are Over

Paul M. Weyrich

Since the early 1990s, the phrase "culture wars" has been used to describe the political conflicts that conservatives and liberals have concerning social issues, morals, and cultural values. In the following viewpoint, originally published in 1999, Paul M. Weyrich contends that liberal ideology and political correctness have taken over American society and are leading to a dramatic cultural disintegration. Maintaining that conservatives have failed to implement a political agenda that would protect the country's traditional values, Weyrich advises conservatives to "drop out" of American culture and refocus their energies away from politics. Conservatives should develop new institutions to preserve Judeo-Christian civilization even as the surrounding culture collapses, he concludes. Weyrich, a longtime conservative activist, is the founding president of the Heritage Foundation.

As you read, consider the following questions:
1. According to Weyrich, what two assumptions have guided the conservative agenda during the past two decades?
2. What is "cultural Marxism," in the author's opinion?
3. In what specific ways can conservatives work to preserve traditional cultural values, according to Weyrich?

Paul M. Weyrich, "Q: Should Conservatives Refocus Their Energies Away from Politics? Yes: They Should Form New Institutions That Are Impervious to 'Cultural Marxism,'" *Insight*, vol. 15, March 29, 1999, pp. 24, 26. Copyright © 1999 by News World Communications, Inc. Reproduced by permission.

A 1998 speech to the Conservative Leadership Conference provided the chance for some different (some would say radical) thinking on the state of the conservative movement. Rather than simply analyze the recent elections or comment on the congressional agenda, I believe it is time for a more fundamental review of the core premises on which the movement has operated.

For at least the last two decades, conservatives have operated on one factual and one strategic assumption. First, the factual assumption that a majority of Americans basically agrees with our point of view is what led me to recommend that the Rev. Jerry Falwell call his organization the "Moral Majority." Second, the strategic assumption has been that electing conservatives to Congress and helping them achieve leadership positions would lead to implementing our agenda.

We have pursued the strategic plan with some success. The history of conservative politics—from the defeat of Robert Taft in 1952 to the nomination of Barry Goldwater to the election of Ronald Reagan to the takeover of Congress by the Republican Party in 1994—indeed shows that conservatives have learned to succeed in getting our people elected.

Why, then, did that not lead to implementing our agenda? The reason is that politics itself has proven insufficient because of the collapse of the culture within which it operates. That culture is becoming an ever-widening sewer that simply has overwhelmed politics.

As a result, we must rethink what we who still believe in our traditional, Western, Judeo-Christian culture—whether we are a majority or not—can and should do under these circumstances. Yes, pursuing politics is important. Trying to retake existing cultural institutions that have been captured by the other side is important. But these no longer can be the only fronts in this war.

The Ideology of Political Correctness

The United States is fast becoming an ideological state. The ideology of Political Correctness, which openly calls for the destruction of our traditional culture, has gripped the body politic and other institutions, including even the church. It has completely taken over the academic community and thoroughly pervades the entertainment industry. Indeed, that ideology threatens literally to control every aspect of our lives.

Political Correctness, more accurately called "cultural Marxism," is part of a deliberate plan. Its history has been documented elsewhere, but suffice it to say that the United States is very close to becoming a state totally dominated by this ideology, one that is bitterly hostile to Western culture. As a result, people for the first time in American history must be afraid of what they say. If they say the "wrong thing," they suddenly can have legal or political problems, even lose their jobs or be expelled from college. Open discussion and telling the truth about certain topics is discouraged or punished by branding decent and rational people as "racist," "sexist," "homophobic," "insensitive" or "judgmental."

Since Political Correctness is overwhelming the very politics to which conservatives looked for cultural victories, what can we do? Let me be perfectly frank about it. A real moral majority would have driven Bill Clinton out of office. While Republicans' lack of political will is part of the problem, more powerful is the fact that most Americans tolerate, and even celebrate, what only a few years ago they would have found intolerable. We no longer can make excuses or repeat clichés and slogans when, for example, a simple ban on partial-birth abortion fails at the polls in Washington state and Colorado. Developments such as these demonstrate that a moral majority no longer exists in America.

Avoiding the Cultural Fallout

We probably have lost the overall culture war, which explains why even winning in politics does not lead to cultural victories. Avoiding the resulting fallout requires separating from the institutions that have fallen victim to cultural Marxism. Taking a cue from Christian history, the word "holy" means "set apart" and those whose beliefs were in the minority often worked to preserve the culture while the surrounding society disintegrated. One modern example of such separation is the homeschooling movement. The homeschoolers have seceded from public schools that condition students rather than educate them and have created parallel institutions in their own homes.

We must pursue a whole series of similar opportunities for bypassing altogether the institutions controlled by the enemies of Western culture. Fighting on their "turf" will be exhausting and ultimately lead to failure. Ending up in the right place requires starting in the right place, and a strategy of separation has much more to do with who we are and what we will become.

The Left Has Won the Culture War

In *Slouching Towards Gomorrah*, Judge Robert Bork makes the claim that "Decline runs across our entire culture." Having described a book-burning at Yale, Bork concludes with the comment, "The charred books on the sidewalk in New Haven were a metaphor, a symbol of the coming torching of America's intellectual and moral capital by the barbarians of modern liberalism." Alas, the barbarians are at the gates, and, despite an occasional cultural victory by the Right, any realistic assessment of American cultural life today must acknowledge that the Left has utterly triumphed in the *kulturkampf* [culture war].

Herbert London, *American Outlook*, Spring 1998.

Another example is the boycott against Disney led by the Southern Baptists, Focus on the Family and other Christian leaders. On the one hand, some might look at Disney's profits and say the boycott has failed. On the other hand, a separation strategy would focus on the many people who otherwise would have been poisoned by Disney's antireligious "entertainment." They scored a victory by separating themselves from some of the cultural rot and devoting their resources elsewhere.

The degree to which Americans, and especially young people, have absorbed this decadent culture without even understanding that they are a part of it is truly shocking. Working to mitigate the damage by separating from this hostile culture is possible without becoming Amish or moving to a bunker somewhere. If there is no vaccine against a threatening disease, quarantine may be the only hope.

Politicians who talk only of technological developments or the Dow Jones industrial average are liars. We are not in the dawn of a new civilization, but the twilight of an old one, and we may escape its demise with mere remnants of the great Judeo-Christian civilization that we have known down through the ages.

Consider a variation of the radical slogans of the 1960s. First, turn off. Turn off the television and video games and some of the garbage on the Internet. Turn off the avenues for consuming cultural decadence. Second, tune out. Create a little stillness. In the former Soviet Union, it is impossible to escape the pounding beat of Western rock music. If that is America's cultural export, it is no wonder some Russians are becoming anti-American. Third, drop out. Drop out of this culture and find places, even if in the sanctity of your own home, to educate your children and live godly, righteous and sober lives.

The assumptions of the last two decades no longer are valid. The record shows that the culture has decayed into something approaching barbarism even while we chalked up victories on the political battlefield. Perhaps this means the cart of politics has been put before the horse of culture. If that is so, we need to take a fresh look, find a different strategy and open a new front. There simply is too much at stake to cover our ears and insist otherwise.

"The main goal [of religious right activists] is still to reclaim mainstream culture and eventually regain political power."

The Culture Wars Are Not Over

People for the American Way

People for the American Way (PFAW) is a nonprofit foundation that opposes the political agenda of the religious right. In the following viewpoint, PFAW argues that conservatives—particularly the religious right—have not abandoned America's culture wars. Although right-wing activist Paul Weyrich publicly declared a defeat in the culture wars and called on conservatives to give up efforts to promote their agenda by political means, the actions of most conservative activists suggest otherwise. The religious right is still pursuing its efforts to influence elections and retrieve political power, PFAW concludes.

As you read, consider the following questions:

1. According to People for the American Way, what 1999 incident set off a major debate among conservatives?
2. What is minister D. James Kennedy's opinion on the culture wars, according to the authors?
3. In the opinion of PFAW, what is the specific purpose of the Committee to Restore American Values?

In mid-February 1999, shortly after the Senate acquittal of President Bill Clinton, Heritage Foundation founder and current head of Coalitions for America, Paul Weyrich, declared that "[p]olitics itself had failed." The people he once termed the "moral majority" should "drop out of this culture, and find places . . . where we can live godly, righteous and sober lives." Weyrich posted his message in an open letter on the website of the Free Congress Foundation, the Washington-based political group he heads. Weyrich's very public renunciation of the political arena set off a major debate in the right-wing political movement. Many national right-wing figures responded by calmly but quickly refuting his arguments.

Larry Arnn of the Claremont Institute and Ed Feulner of the Heritage Foundation wrote in the March 16th, 1999, *Los Angeles Times* that Weyrich's "strategy will lead to disaster" and that conservatives "should not allow impatience for final victory to cloud their judgement."

The Family Research Council's (FRC) executive vice-president responded by promising to "fight another 20, 40, 60 years—whatever it may take." FRC also tried to provide a counter to Weyrich's message by running ads on 200 radio stations urging conservatives to call Congress and "voice your values so Congress will value your voice." Gary Bauer, who [had] recently left FRC to pursue the GOP presidential nomination, called dropping out "a silly idea."

D. James Kennedy of Coral Ridge Ministries quickly rebuked those who held the view that Religious Right activists should withdraw from the public arena. "To those who say that the culture war is over, I say, 'We have not yet begun to fight!'" said Kennedy to an audience at his "Reclaiming America for Christ" conference in February 1999. In case anyone is worried that Kennedy's patience will wear thin, he assured one interviewer that "In any war, there are times when it seems like you are losing. It's not going to be over in 2000 or 2004 or 2006 or 2008 or 2010. We're in this for the long haul."

Religious Right radio host and 1996 Republican Presidential candidate Alan Keyes also disagreed, telling Weyrich to "Cheer up" in a column on the right-wing WorldNet-Daily website. Weighing in on Weyrich's side was Howard

Phillips, the head of the Conservative Caucus and the U.S Taxpayer's Party candidate for President in 1996.

The Moral Majority's Down Side

The public feuding started by Weyrich's open letter was heightened by the release of a book that provides a more introspective critique of the Religious Right political movement.

Syndicated columnist Cal Thomas and Baptist minister Ed Dobson have written a book titled *Blinded by Might* in which they criticize the core ideas behind the Moral Majority and the Christian Coalition. Formerly involved with the Moral Majority, Thomas and Dobson argue that American society should be improved by changing individuals not politics, and that conservative Christians have been tainted by their involvement in politics. The authors now say that they see the down side of the Moral Majority's political involvement—an unhealthy focus on media coverage and fundraising.

Thomas and Dobson have been sharply criticized by some on the right since they went public with their critique. D. James Kennedy withdrew an invitation for Thomas to

---

Right-Wing Organizations

The Eagle Forum, led by Phyllis Schlafly, almost single-handedly defeated the Equal Rights Amendment (ERA) and is still around. *Exodus International* is an organization that claims to have converted thousands of gay men and lesbians to heterosexuality. *Family Life Ministries*, led by Tim LaHaye, seeks to save America from secular humanism. LaHaye, of course, was formerly a Moral Majority leader. *The National Right to Life Committee* opposes abortion and women's reproductive freedom. *Rockford Institute* in Illinois opposes the erosion of traditional values resulting from an increasingly pluralistic society, so it sees multiculturalism as the enemy. *The Traditional Values Coalition* is active in anti-homosexual legislation and opposes even school-based counselling programs for gay and lesbian teenagers. *Scriptures for America* is really out there on the Right. It's a racist, anti-semitic group. It espouses Christian identity theology, which claims that Anglo-Saxons are the Bible's true chosen people and Jews are interlopers! They also believe gay people should be executed.

Virginia Ramey Mollenkott, *The Witness*, October 1996.

---

speak at the Reclaiming America for Christ conference, Jerry Falwell said in a news release that he would not discuss the book, and James Dobson (no relation) reportedly sent the authors a note effectively saying don't call me again. Said Kennedy, "I'm fighting for God and for truth and for morality and for decency. When we quit doing these things we might as well lay down and die."

The Right Will Not Abandon Politics

Paul Weyrich's polemic, followed by the publication of the Dobson/Thomas book, sparked widespread speculation about whether the Religious Right's troops would heed Weyrich's call. In fact all of the squabbling and the subsequent media coverage might lead one to believe that Religious Right activists were preparing to abandon political activity. A closer examination suggests just the opposite. The movement is gearing up to work harder than ever to advance its agenda during future elections. . . .

These are not the signs of a movement that is ready to throw in the towel. . . .

Just a few days before he posted his open letter Weyrich himself announced plans to rally support for the House managers who prosecuted President Clinton in the Senate impeachment trial. Representatives Tom DeLay and Henry Hyde are among those to be awarded the Free Congress Foundation's "Liberty Award" for their "efforts to try to save America." Furthermore, Weyrich and other Religious Right heavyweights such as Phyllis Schlafly, Randy Tate and Mike Farris have formed the Committee to Restore American Values. The purpose of this ad-hoc group is to pick a successful right-wing Republican presidential candidate who can galvanize the Religious Right vote in 2000.

Weyrich has also expanded on his initial statement. After days of constant interviews and talk show appearances, Weyrich issued a commentary saying, "We are not talking about dropping out of politics. We are talking about recognizing that, in terms of culture, politics is not going to get us where we need to go." For Weyrich, a polluted culture requires a kind of Christian separatism, but the main goal is still to reclaim mainstream culture and eventually regain political power.

*"The White House [has] a close alliance
with the Religious Right in the nation's
war over values."*

The Right Is Intensifying the Culture Wars

Jim Whittle

The religious right is stepping up its plans to promote its political and cultural agenda in the United States, reports freelance writer Jim Whittle in the following viewpoint. Moreover, because Republican leaders are eager to find ways to
attract conservative Christian voters, the religious right has a
strong influence on President George W. Bush's administration. Right-wing organizations are working closely with the
Bush administration to oppose gay rights, denounce reproductive rights, loosen the separation of church and state, and
appoint conservative Supreme Court Justices, Whittle asserts.

As you read, consider the following questions:

1. What is the Family Research Council, according to
   Whittle?
2. According to the author, why did James Dobson give
   George W. Bush a D minus on a bipartisan education
   bill?
3. Why was the group American Renewal formed,
   according to Whittle?

Jim Whittle, "All in the Family: Top Bush Administration Leaders, Religious
Right Lieutenants Plot Strategy in Culture 'War,'" *Church & State*, vol. 55, May
2002, pp. 4–7. Copyright © 2002 by Americans United for Separation of Church
and State. Reproduced by permission.

White House political strategist Karl Rove sounded like a general addressing his troops. "We need to find ways to win the war," Rove said. "This is a gigantic war with a whole series of battles that need to be fought. And what you all do every day is win important skirmishes a yard at a time."

But President George W. Bush's top adviser wasn't talking about the war on terrorism. He was talking about the White House's close alliance with the Religious Right in the nation's war over values.

Speaking to the Family Research Council's (FRC) 2002 Washington Briefing, Rove assured a gathering of key Religious Right activists from around the country that the Bush administration shares their views on issues such as granting tax aid to churches, restricting abortion, opposing gay rights laws, promoting marriage and appointing "conservative" judges.

It was a speech that spoke volumes about the ongoing influence of the Religious Right in America. With the Christian Coalition fading as a political force, Republican political leaders are turning to other Religious Right organizations to plot strategy and lure conservative Christian voters into their column. These days, the Family Research Council is moving to the front of the pack as a savvy lobbying group that plays partisan hardball.

The Washington, D.C.–based outfit has an annual budget of over $10 million, a grassroots network of contacts around the country and, perhaps most importantly, the ardent backing of James Dobson, the radio counselor who sparked the FRC's formation and gives its leaders a nationwide audience whenever the political situation warrants.

The group's agenda is decidedly hostile to the separation of church and state. FRC's goal, said its president Kenneth L. Connor, is "to help the family in our country and to advance a society that is informed with a Judeo-Christian world view and that reflects in the final analysis the sovereignty of the Lord over all aspects of our daily life."

The FRC's influence in the Bush White House shows in the guest list drawn to its annual briefing. In addition to Rove, other administration figures included Secretary of Housing and Urban Development (HUD) Mel Martinez, White House Office of Faith-Based and Community Initiatives Chief Jim Towey and White House Deputy Director of Public Liaison Tim Goeglein. . . .

Bush's Appeal to the Religious Right

At the FRC briefing, held in the chandelier-bedecked Crystal Room of the Willard Hotel a few blocks from the White House, Rove ticked off the laundry list of Bush positions sure to make Religious Right hearts beat faster. As activists munched on salmon, roast beef and other delicacies, he appealed for help in winning congressional battles and increasing the Republicans' strength in the Congress.

Rove cited the administration's drive to reauthorize "charitable choice" aid to churches to provide social services, and he touted a White House plan to spend $300 million for state programs to encourage families and marriage. He denounced all forms of human cloning and said he was "shocked" when the Orthodox Jews announced support for therapeutic cloning. He called support for that position "morally reprehensible to anybody who cares about life.". . .

Rove also touted "crisis pregnancy centers"—religiously motivated agencies that encourage pregnant women not to have abortions—as "fabulous defenders of life." He said the administration is looking for ways to assist the centers with equipment and staffing. . . .

During the question-and-answer session, Rove reiterated Bush's opposition to laws protecting gay people's rights.

"[Bush] believes marriage is between a man and woman, period," observed Rove. "He also believes that we should not carve out special privileges for people on the basis of sexual orientation."

While Rove said Bush would not reject candidates for government posts solely because they are gay, he added, "We've got a culture in our country, particularly a culture that's applauded in this town, that says if it feels good, do it—and better yet, embody it into law. And he doesn't agree with it."

Cementing Ties with Religious Conservatives

Rove concluded with an appeal for the Religious Right to work closely with the Bush administration.

"There will be some times we'll win, and there will be some times we'll lose," he said. "There will be some times you in this room and we over at the White House will find ourselves in agreement, and there will be the occasion when we don't. But we will share a heck of a lot more in common than we don't. And we'll win if we work together far more often than the other side wants us to be. Thank you for what you do in your states. And thank you for what you do for FRC."

The Power-Brokering Christian Right

The Christian right's sway within the Republican Party, along with its far-reaching grassroots base, made it an influential power broker in the neck-and-neck 2000 presidential race. During the primary, mainstream pundits scoffed at candidate George W. Bush for naming Jesus as his favorite philosopher. But if that was a political calculation on Bush's part (as much as heartfelt response), it was quite possibly among the savviest of his campaign. From that moment on, the powerful Republican evangelical bloc has remained solidly at his side. Republican evangelical voters—80 percent of whom voted for Bush, compared with only 65 percent for Bob Dole in 1996—were crucial to getting Bush into office.

Unlike his father, Bush was quick to make good on that support. Shortly after his inauguration in 2001, Bush cut off funds for organizations providing abortion services overseas (the announcement perfectly coincided with a "march for life" in downtown Washington). As director of the U.S. Office of Personnel Management, overseeing the entire federal workforce, Bush appointed the former dean of the government school at Pat Robertson's Regent University, Kay Coles James, who also happens to be one of the nation's most articulate anti-abortion advocates. And most notably, to the United States's top law-enforcement post he named John Ashcroft, a Pentecostal whose insistence on holding daily prayer sessions in his Justice Department office has earned him the scorn of Beltway pundits and the adulation of the Christian right. Ashcroft's attempt to overturn Oregon's assisted-suicide law was similarly popular with evangelical activists.

Nina J. Easton, *American Prospect*, May 20, 2002.

The other administration officials at the meeting also sounded themes designed to cement Bush's ties with religious conservatives. HUD Secretary Martinez, for example, stressed guidelines he has issued encouraging churches to take advantage of federal housing grants and permitting religious displays and activities in publicly funded developments. He even included a reading of Psalm 37.

Towey, chief of the "faith-based" office, took a similar approach, dismissing constitutional objections to government funding of church-based social services as "foolishness." He argued that the Supreme Court is moving away from a "strict separation" approach to church-state separation, and said he thinks the justices will approve the Ohio voucher scheme that funds religious schools. . . .

Seeking Policy Victories

At the Washington gathering, Religious Right activists reflected strong support for Bush, but disappointment that he has not taken a harder line on social issues. FRC Vice President for Government Affairs Connie Mackey told the crowd that FRC activists and their allies are sprinkled throughout the government. But that doesn't always translate into easy policy victories.

"I love 'em and I hate 'em," groused Mackey about the administration. "I could just kill them sometimes, because we know what they need to do and they don't always do it our way."

She continued, however, "Lobbying works now from both ends of Pennsylvania Avenue and everything in between—that means all the federal agencies. The good news is that with President Bush in office a lot of FRC people are in place. And that's the good part that makes our life a lot easier."

Dobson, an FRC board member, displayed a similar spirit in a dialogue with FRC president Connor. Asked what he thought of the Bush administration, Dobson replied, "Compared to what? Compared to his predecessor?"

"We have reason," said Dobson, "to be very, very thankful, I think,—now this is in my own statement and it almost sounds political and I don't mean it that way—but thankful that George Bush is in the White House. I'm very thankful for those 350 votes in Florida. You just think, my goodness, we could be dealing with Albert Gore at this time. And I shudder to think what would have happened on 9-11 if he had been in the White House."

However, Dobson added, "His administration is not ideologically committed to everything we are obviously. I know that you feel, Ken, and I don't know if you have shared this, you have to push on them a little bit to get them to do the right thing."

Calling the administration's record "mixed but mostly positive," he praised Bush's marriage advocacy but blasted the bipartisan education bill, giving Bush a "D-" on the subject. The bill, he said, did not include vouchers for religious schools and it gave more power to the National Education Association, which he denounced for supporting the "homosexual agenda."

Dobson remains obsessed with the gay issue. He told the crowd, "Without question in my mind, the greatest danger to our moral perspective and to the family and indeed to the nation is the homosexual activist movement."

"Homosexuals want it all," he charged. "They want everything. . . . They want it all, and what's scary about it is they're getting it all."

Blasting "Liberal" Positions

Operating from his Colorado-based Focus on the Family empire, Dobson lobs rhetorical shells at administration leaders when they stray into "liberal" positions. After Secretary of State Colin Powell encouraged condom use for sexually active teenagers during an interview on MTV, Dobson unleashed his radio listeners in a telephone barrage on the White House. Dobson took credit when Bush quickly reemphasized his support for abstinence education programs a few days after the Powell remarks.

At the FRC event, Dobson asked Rove to thank the president for his courage in contradicting Powell.

"It didn't take courage, it just took conviction," Rove replied. "He wasn't rebuking the secretary of state. He was just making clear what the policy of this administration was with clarity. Sometimes people are going to say things and be off tune a little bit, but the president will make certain that people understand clearly where the administration is coming from by word and deed."

Courting the Far Right

In order to keep the pressure on the Republican Party leadership to conform to their agenda, Dobson and his allies at FRC continue a courtship with figures on the political far right. A featured speaker at the Washington briefing was Pat Buchanan, the fiery right-wing pundit whose third-party candidacy for president could easily have tilted the 2000 election to Democrat Al Gore by siphoning off conservative voters.

Buchanan, author of a new book *The Death of the West*, railed against immigration from Mexico and other Third World countries, declining birth rates in the United States and other Western countries, weakening influence for Christianity and secular humanist control of the public schools, and charged that the GOP "raised the white flag in the culture war" at its convention in 2000.

Although critics see his message as intolerant, racist and xenophobic, Buchanan remains intensely popular with many in the FRC crowd. He received enthusiastic applause when introduced and at the end of his remarks. "You're my hero," one man gushed, during the question-and-answer period. But Buchanan's harsh anti-immigrant, anti-Hispanic rhetoric didn't set well with some Religious Right strategists.

Tom Minnery, a top official of Dobson's Focus on the Family, chided Buchanan for his anti-Hispanic swipes. He noted that Hispanic Catholics in California are sympathetic to the Religious Right agenda on "family" issues and played a key role in blocking gay rights proposals in the legislature recently. FRC, meanwhile, has hired a full-time staffer to cultivate the Hispanic community.

This shows that FRC leaders, unlike unsophisticated Religious Right leaders of the past, are politically savvy and pragmatic, studying and responding to demographic changes and relying on focus groups to craft their message. They also play political hardball.

FRC is a 501(c)(3) tax-exempt organization that is limited by the IRS Code in the kinds of political activities it can conduct. As a result, FRC leaders have created a companion group, American Renewal—with a 501(c)(4) tax classification—to wage its more overt political crusades. Connor, an unsuccessful Republican gubernatorial candidate from Florida who followed Gary Bauer as head of FRC, serves as president of both groups.

American Renewal

At the FRC meeting, Connor said American Renewal exists because some politicians need to feel the heat before they see the light. He jokingly introduced the unit's executive director, Richard Lessner, as "the hammer."

Insisting that politicians operate mostly out of fear of losing reelection, Lessner said, "We need to twist arms and stomp our feet and sometimes kick up some dust to make them do what they may not want to do. . . . It's who's able to bring the most pressure to bear against the politicians at any particular time that's going to win the battle. So American Renewal is sort of the pointy end of the spear, if you will, for FRC."

He boasted about American Renewal's well-publicized media assault on Senate Majority Leader Tom Daschle (D-S.D.). Lessner's unit, in conjunction with the Dobson-allied South Dakota Family Council, ran advertisements in South Dakota newspapers accusing the Democratic senator of helping Iraqi dictator Saddam Hussein.

Under a picture of Saddam, the ad asked, "Why is America buying 725,000 barrels of oil a day from this man?" Under a picture of Daschle, it answered, "Because this man won't let America drill for oil at home."

The ad charged that Daschle was blocking a Bush administration energy bill that would allow oil exploration in the Alaska Arctic National Wildlife Refuge.

Some news media observers saw the ad as a cheap shot and a clear example of dirty politics, but the FRC briefing crowd wildly cheered Lessner's comments about it.

Calling Daschle "one of the main obstructions we have in Washington right now," Lessner said "we are going to make him feel some pain and pay a price for his obstructionist tactics."

At a minimum, the anti-Daschle ad campaign reinforces the partisan character of American Renewal—and its parent group, the FRC.

Although Lessner noted that his operation has also sent

one mailing criticizing Sen. Orrin Hatch (R-Utah) for failing to support a strict ban on cloning, the overwhelming majority of American Renewal's work has been on behalf of Republicans. During the 2000 elections, statement after statement bashed the Democratic Party platform and candidates Gore and Joe Lieberman. American Renewal pushed for Bush's victory in the post-election confusion and campaigned hard for the confirmation of John Ashcroft as attorney general.

Partisanship at the FRC briefing was pervasive. For example, Daniel Lapin, an ultraconservative rabbi who often speaks at Religious Right gatherings, told the crowd he isn't comfortable declaring that the Republicans are "the party of God," but he is sure that "today the Democratic Party is evil and destructive.". . .

Connor, Dobson and company now are gearing up for what they view as the most important battle of all—the fight to get right-wing nominees on the U.S. Supreme Court who will reverse rulings upholding church-state separation, reproductive rights and related concerns. While these Religious Right figures may have quibbles with the Bush administration over an issue here or there, all will be forgiven if hard-right nominees are placed on the high court.

Insisting that all important family and moral issues are decided by the justices, Dobson said the first Supreme Court nominee is "a critical moment."

"If Christians don't get off their backsides and let our voices be heard on that one," he warned, "we're going to get rolled again."

When that moment comes, Dobson and the other forces of the Religious Right will be ready. Those who support church-state separation and individual rights will have to be ready too.

"We're in for a long-term cultural battle in which neither side gains total victory."

Neither the Right Nor the Left Can Win the Culture Wars

Stanley Kurtz

In the following viewpoint, Stanley Kurtz maintains that the liberal-versus-conservative culture wars are ongoing, despite suggestions by some political activists that conservatives had lost the culture wars. Although conservatives have suffered setbacks, the liberal agenda for American culture is untenable, argues Kurtz. Ultimately, most Americans cannot accept the radical erosion of traditional values that left-wing activists promote. When the left breaks mainstream taboos, a traditionalist reaction inevitably ensues—resulting in a constant oscillation between radicalism and conservatism. Neither the left nor the right will become the ultimate victor in this cultural battle, the author concludes. Kurtz is a research fellow at Stanford University's Hoover Institution and a contributing editor at *National Review Online*.

As you read, consider the following questions:
1. According to Kurtz, what events led some right-wingers to conclude that conservatives had lost the culture wars?
2. What recent cultural battles offer proof that the left-wing agenda is unsustainable, in the author's opinion?
3. In Kurtz's view, how do Americans really feel about homosexuality and feminism?

Stanley Kurtz, "Push-Pull: The Way the Culture War Works, Unendingly," *National Review*, vol. 53, March 5, 2001. Copyright © 2001 by National Review, Inc. Reproduced by permission.

P olitical correctness often succeeds by creating the illu- sion that no other points of view exist. Go to a book- store, for example, in a tony liberal neighborhood, and you will see that books by, say, [conservatives] Rush Limbaugh and Bill O'Reilly are not displayed prominently (as would befit their best-seller status), but filed away on the shelves. When is a best-seller not a best-seller? When it contains views the P.C. crowd would like to wish away.

The ultimate expression of this desire to erase the other side may be the oft-heard claim that the culture war is over, and that conservatives lost. After the Republican love-fest in Philadelphia [the Republican national convention in 2000], with Pat Buchanan gone and social conservatism invisible, the culture war was supposed to be finished. But ever since the appearance of that blue-red map of the Al Gore and Bush nations, the persistence of our social divide has become inescapable. Indeed, President George W. Bush's under- standing of the indispensable role of social conservatives in his coalition is what led to the current culture clash over At- torney General John Ashcroft.

A Long-Term Cultural Battle

So the culture war didn't disappear after all. The talk about a permanent conservative defeat does signal a significant social change; but what has changed is only that moral assumptions formerly taken for granted have now been put on the table for discussion. They are being discussed, but have not been finally decided. Conservatives can no longer expect majority agreement with their cultural views, but the Left has a prob- lem too: Its cultural program is too utopian to shape a stable, coherent society. That means we're in for a long-term cul- tural battle in which neither side gains total victory.

Once the hippies and antiwar activists began their long march through the institutions, war was inevitable. By 1996, talk of conservative defeat had begun. The Left chafed at the Republican Congress and Clintonian triangulation in poli- tics, but consoled itself with a declaration of victory in the culture: The academy and the media were now firmly in its grip. Gay Day at Disney World, the failure of William Ben- nett to make a dent in Hollywood, and the tepid public reaction to Madonna's out-of-wedlock child—all were taken as signs that the Right had finally lost the cultural battle. But the crucial moment for conservatives came in early 1999, with President Bill Clinton's acquittal in the Senate. Clinton's victory led conservative activist Paul Weyrich to declare, "I no longer believe that there is a moral majority." Weyrich warned of "a cultural collapse of historic proportions, a collapse so great that it simply overwhelms politics."

Jubilant liberals seized on Weyrich's concession as proof of conservative surrender, but both sides were confusing the collapse of an unequivocally traditional majority with the end of the culture war. Yes, social conservatives have suffered a serious setback: Anything approaching unanimity on cultural questions no longer exists. But the weakness of the Left's alternative makes its own ultimate victory unlikely. In the late Sixties and early Seventies, all the utopian experiments fell apart owing to their own incoherence. Sexual liberation ran aground on the shoals of jealousy, male/female difference, and the needs of children. Communal sharing and collective identity were irreconcilable with individual liberty. Group solidarities splintered indefinitely into subgroups, and this led to paralysis. Turning the personal into the political made for intrusive tyranny.

Left-Wing Culture Is Unsustainable

This same incoherent utopianism remains embedded in the cultural program of the Left. The culture of the Sixties is basically unsustainable: It can only live parasitically, on the body of tradition. Each victory for the new morality can only lead to yet more radical—and less realistic—demands, eventually provoking a traditionalist reaction.

Take homosexuality. It's true that America's view of homosexuality has shifted irrevocably. Only a small minority of today's Americans would have us return to the Fifties, when homosexuality was so shameful that gays were barred from positions in the State Department for fear of blackmail. Still, although many Americans welcome increased tolerance of gays, most would nonetheless object to full equivalence between homosexuality and heterosexuality—that's why majorities continue to oppose gay marriage. But complete removal of any distinction between homosexuality and hetero-sexuality remains the program of gay activists. In the end, this would require not so much gay marriage, as the complete elimination of state-sanctioned marriage in favor of an infinitely variable set of family and sexual arrangements. And, as we're beginning to see in a few states, total equivalence would also require secondary-school programs in which homosexuality and heterosexuality are presented to children as equally legitimate alternatives.

A War of Ideas

Most Americans—wisely, in my view—do not normally pre-occupy themselves with developments in the political and in-tellectual landscape, and for them the notion that the nation is caught up in a culture war is indeed alien and unpersuasive. But those who, for better or worse, find it their business to deal with ideas cannot but be aware that such a conflict is in fact in progress.

It rages among the cultural elites, and it is in deadly earnest. It involves competing worldviews that, however subtle and complex in their details, can nonetheless be summed up with rough accuracy under such encompassing rubrics as "pro-gressive" vs. "traditionalist" or "secular" vs. "orthodox." It is essential that the war of ideas be conducted with as much ci-vility as can be mustered, and the search for common ground must never be abandoned. But for those called to be public intellectuals, it is an evasion either to pretend there is no con-flict or to fail to take a stand on contested issues of principle.

James Neuchterlein, *First Things*, October 1999.

Gay activists know all this, and patiently continue to push their radical program—incrementally. But the program is impossible: It rests on the utopian premise that the stigma of homosexuality can be entirely removed, even though that stigma originates in the primal fact that well over 90 percent of the population is heterosexual. Whatever the state does, gays will always feel like outsiders, simply because the vast majority of people take heterosexuality for granted. A mis-guided attempt to "overcome" this preference can only lead to reaction from the heterosexual majority.

This is already happening. As gay "civil unions," and programs on homosexuality directed at high-school students, have been introduced in Sixties-friendly Vermont, conservatives have staged a comeback—handing Republicans control of the state's house for the first time in 14 years. The larger point is that the carriers of the Sixties' cultural legacy will always radicalize their program until it surpasses the limits of possibility and provokes a backlash. So the erosion of the taboo against homosexuality does not mean final cultural victory for the Left; it means perpetual oscillation between radicalism and tradition.

Shifting Values

The impossibility of sustaining a culturally "Left" style of life is also illustrated by voting habits of women after they marry and have children. In ever-increasing numbers, women have been putting off marriage to pursue careers. The abortion right is a valuable safety valve for this lifestyle, so these women tend to vote for pro-choice Democrats. But eventually most women marry, and parenting changes their cultural priorities—moving many into the Republican camp.

Political commentators of different stripes—John Judis in the *New Republic*, David Brooks in the *Weekly Standard*—have spoken of emerging Democratic majorities built around an expanding base of liberal, career-oriented women. But there is an intrinsic limit to the size of any liberal-feminist constituency: the ineradicable yearning of women to marry and mother. If generations of social engineering for androgyny on Israeli kibbutzim could not succeed in moderating these desires, we certainly won't have androgyny in the United States. The impossible utopianism of the feminist drive for androgyny means that, even though the old consensus over "gender" has been broken, what we're in for is perpetual wavering: The trend toward marriage will ebb and flow with changing demographic and social conditions, and the fortunes of the parties will shift accordingly.

Virtually all of the incidents that sparked the Left's declaration of victory in the culture war have in fact had conservative sequels. Eventually, Madonna got married. There may be a Gay Day at Disney World, but the reaction against civil unions in Vermont gives an idea of just how easily a radicalized gay-rights agenda can move blue-collar Democrats into the Republican camp. And Clinton's impeachment drama had a surprising denouement: Al Gore may well have lost because of it. With George W. Bush promising to restore integrity to the White House, Gore was forced to forego Clinton's aid. And for all William Bennett's frustration over Clinton and Hollywood, Gore's most successful move was his choice of Bennett's comrade in arms Joe Lieberman, erstwhile defender of religion and traditional values.

So, the culture wars won't end. With the old consensus broken, but with nothing coherent available to replace it, we're doomed to swing between two unachievable cultural poles. The public is up for grabs. On homosexuality, Americans want neither the intolerance of the Fifties nor the complete equivalence favored by gay activists. On feminism, Americans want the right to dispense with the traditional family—and the right to embrace that tradition when they finally realize how indispensable it is. So not only are there cultural shifts between urban and rural regions, but within the same people at different times in their lives—or even at the same moment, depending on how the question is put.

The intrinsic unworkability of the Left's cultural program means that America's socially conservative opposition will persist. At times, perhaps, it will gain the upper hand; but it will never win total or permanent control. If handled correctly, cultural reaction to Sixties-style extravagance still has the potential to propel Republicans into power. The fortunes of each side will depend on luck and tactical skill. But the arguments over identity, family, and sex are likely to last for generations. The conflicts cut too deep to be wished out of existence by the Left, or solved by the defeatism of the Right. Far from being over, the culture wars have just begun.

*"The conventional wisdom that Americans
are divided into two warring camps
slugging it out over abortion, prayer in
schools, and homosexuality is greatly
exaggerated."*

The Extent of the Culture Wars Has Been Exaggerated

Christian Smith with Michael Emerson, Sally Gallagher,
Paul Kennedy, and David Sikkink

The majority of Americans are not deeply concerned about
culture wars issues, argue Christian Smith and his colleagues
in the following viewpoint. The polarized liberal-versus-
conservative conflicts over such issues as abortion, multiculturalism, and moral values may exist among political activists
and policy makers, but are not of great concern to the general public, the authors contend. Most Americans are more
worried about crime, the economy, and public education,
the authors maintain. Smith is an assistant professor of sociology at the University of North Carolina in Chapel Hill.

As you read, consider the following questions:

1. According to a 1994 poll cited by the authors, what did
   the majority of respondents believe to be the biggest
   problem facing the country?
2. What percentage of all Americans are concerned about
   culture wars issues, according to Smith and his
   colleagues?

Christian Smith with Michael Emerson, Sally Gallagher, Paul Kennedy, and
David Sikkink, "The Myth of Culture Wars: The Case of American
Protestantism," *Cultural Wars in American Politics: Critical Reviews of a Popular
Myth*, edited by Rhys H. Williams. New York: Aldine de Gruyter, 1997.
Copyright © 1997 by Walter de Gruyter, Inc. Reproduced by permission.

Culture wars is a myth. The conventional wisdom that Americans are divided into two warring camps slugging it out over abortion, prayer in schools, and homosexuality is greatly exaggerated. Growing empirical evidence suggests it just is not true. In fact, most Americans are not very invested in culture wars issues. Nor have they taken up oppositional sides with warring "traditionalist" and "progressive" forces to wage their local and national battles. The vast majority of Americans are much more interested in whether their kids learn to read well, whether they can walk their streets safely at night, and whether the government can get the deficit under control than they are in protesting obscene art and gays marching in parades. The important issues for the mass of Americans, in other words, remain economic and social, not cultural-wars issues.

The actual culture wars that we do see on television— shrill fights over abortion, homosexuality, prayer in schools, obscenity in art, and so on—are being waged by a fairly small group of noisy, entrepreneurial activists at the extremes, whose interests are served by the impression that all of America has taken up arms to join their fight. And too many in the academy and the media have cooperated in fostering this perception. But it is a misperception. Most of America is not at war over culture. The Pat Buchanans and Kate Michaelmans of the airwaves have declared war, but very few Americans have shown up for the fight.

How do we know this? We know this because, when one listens more closely to the broad array of ordinary Americans than to the protests and press releases of militant activists, that is what one hears. A wide range of available quantitative and qualitative evidence from opinion polls and in-depth research interviews tells us that the majority of Americans are simply not very interested in culture wars.

Countless hours of media programming covering controversies surrounding Operation Rescue, Pat Robertson's presidential race, multiculturalism in schools, the Mapplethorpe exhibits, gay pride parades, vulgar "gangsta rap" lyrics, *The Last Temptation of Christ*, antiabortion shootings, and Ralph Reed and the Christian Coalition would suggest that a national culture war is tearing America apart. One would think that most Americans are ever arming for battle, ever mobilizing for the next demonstration, blockade, hearing, protest, debate, and rally. Thankfully, that is not so. In fact, these books, articles, and broadcasts have together far overblown the story. This viewpoint is an attempt to help put matters back into perspective.

What's Bothering America?

The first bit of evidence that should cause us to suspect the culture wars story are the answers that people give to questions about America's problems. Political scientists and pollsters who conduct surveys frequently ask the question, What do you think is the biggest problem facing America today? The results are instructive. Most people say things like the federal deficit, crime, unemployment, health care, poverty, and racism. Somewhere down the list you find a few people saying moral decline. People almost never mention abortion, multiculturalism, prayer in schools, secular humanism, the imposition of the Christian Right agenda, pornography, or homosexuality.

For example, a 1994 poll of 1,492 Americans asked, "What do you feel are the two or three biggest problems facing the country today?" Forty-two percent of respondents— who were asked to name two or three problems—said crime was the biggest problem. Twenty percent said unemployment and low wages, 19 percent health care costs, 18 percent drug abuse, 15 percent poverty and homelessness, 12 percent poor education, 10 percent the economy, 9 percent bad government, and 9 percent the federal deficit. All answers regarding ethical problems in society, moral decline, the decline of religion, and pornography were combined into one "immorality" category, which garnered a mere 8 percent. Only 1 percent mentioned teenage pregnancy, and less than 0.5 percent mentioned abortion. Nobody said prayer in schools, secular humanism, threats to civil liberties, multiculturalism, or any of the other contentious and highly publicized culture wars issues.

Even when the question is asked differently, the results are the same. A 1995 Harris poll of 1,004 Americans, for example, asked, "What do you think are the two most important issues for the government to address?" Twenty-two percent reported crime and violence, 18 percent the federal deficit, 16 percent health care, 14 percent welfare, 10 percent taxes, 10 percent education, 8 percent each for programs for the poor, the economy, and programs for the elderly, 7 percent unemployment, and 6 percent foreign policy issues. Only 4 percent mentioned morality and sex on television, 2 percent abortion, 2 percent the decline of family values, and 1 percent the decline of religion. Not an overwhelming interest in culture wars issues here.

Examples could be multiplied, but one final case should suffice. A 1989 *Washington Post* survey of 1,009 Americans asked, "When you think about the future of our country and the next generation, what things concern you the most?" Respondents were allowed to name two issues. Twenty-five percent said they were concerned about drugs. Fifteen percent said the threat of war, 14 percent the environment, 13 percent the economy, 12 percent crime and violence, 9 percent unemployment, and 9 percent education. Nine percent said they were concerned about moral decline, 2 percent ethics, 1 percent the lack of religion, and 1 percent abortion.

It is possible to salvage the culture wars story even in the face of these survey results. One could argue that people view crime and welfare, for example, as the results of a serious moral decline, which itself must be reversed through culture wars. One wonders, however, why, if moral decline were the perceived root cause of these problems, more people would not simply report moral decline as the biggest problem facing America. On the other hand, one might argue that, although survey respondents really do believe things like abortion and school prayer are the most important issues, either they think that is not what the survey researchers want to hear, or they are reluctant to state views they think are socially undesirable. However—aside from the fact that some respondents *did* think it okay to mention abortion and immorality—if this is so, it speaks volumes about people's convictions and militancy on these matters.

Although one would not want to base an entire case on these opinion data alone, it does tell us something. It tells us that the issues that really interest the vast majority of Americans are economic and social issues, not the much-ballyhooed culture wars issues. And though it is clear that some Americans *are* concerned about what might be thought of as culture wars issues, extrapolating their numbers from these kinds of polls shows that they represent no more than 4 or 5 percent of all Americans. . . .

David Moore gives us another perspective in his April/May 1995 article in *The Public Perspective*, which uses survey data to identify the magnitude of the Religious Right. According to Moore, if you define the Religious Right as politically conservative independent or Republican Christians who say that religion is very important in their lives, who attend church services regularly, and who oppose abortion in all circumstances, then the Religious Right makes up only 4 percent of the American population, and only 9 percent of Republicans. Not exactly half of a nation torn in two.

In her award-winning 1986 book, *Cities on a Hill*, Frances FitzGerald described Jerry Falwell's Moral Majority as "a disciplined, charging army." That image lives on today, as conventional wisdom frames and frets about the Pat Robertsons, Ralph Reeds, Pat Buchanans, Randall Terrys, and James Dobsons of the world. We would like to suggest, however, that when you stop listening to these noisy, entrepreneurial elites for a moment, and begin listening to the great mass of ordinary Americans, particularly to those within the institution of American Protestantism, you don't hear the clamor of a disciplined charging army. You hear the struggles and worries of regular folks trying to get along in a world that seems to them increasingly dangerous and dysfunctional. You hear people worried about their kids, about the economy, about their neighborhoods. You hear people often trying to follow God as best they know how. To most of these folks with these concerns, the brouhaha over culture wars is fairly distant and trivial.

Culture wars among some elites do exist. But the story that has been told about them has been quite overblown. Perhaps by putting matters back into perspective, the voices of ordinary Americans can help to refocus national attention on pressing issues: on matters of economic justice, fiscal responsibility, racial reconciliation, environmental stewardship, and support for the kind of stable, nurturing families that nearly all Americans so desperately desire.

"[Cultural Creatives] want to carry forward what is valuable from the past and integrate it with what's needed for the future."

A New Counterculture Is Emerging

Paul H. Ray and Sherry Ruth Anderson

In the following viewpoint, Paul H. Ray and Sherry Ruth Anderson contend that a new American subculture may find healthy ways to merge conservative and progressive ideals. Described as "cultural creatives," this new subculture refuses to take sides in the culture wars, hoping instead to develop a movement that integrates the best of the "traditional" (conservative) and "modern" (moderate to liberal) value systems. The authors maintain that the cultural creatives' respect for idealism, spirituality, and diversity makes them the group most likely to bring about positive changes in U.S. society and culture. Sociologist Ray and psychologist Anderson are the authors of *The Cultural Creatives: How 50 Million People Are Changing the World*, from which this viewpoint is excerpted.

As you read, consider the following questions:

1. How does James Davison Hunter, quoted by the authors, define the culture war?
2. How do Traditionals define "values relativism," in the authors' opinion?
3. According to Ray and Anderson, what is the downside of modernism?

"Politics itself has failed. And politics has failed because of the collapse of the culture," Paul Weyrich, an architect of right-wing strategies, wrote in 1999 in a widely quoted public letter following President Bill Clinton's impeachment. The culture we are living in, Weyrich claimed, is becoming "an ever-wider sewer." His voice was extreme, but other prominent conservatives have also worried aloud about a general moral decline in American culture. Henry Hyde, the House Judiciary Committee chairman who led the prosecution team against Mr. Clinton, told senators toward the end of the trial, "I wonder if, after this culture war is over . . . an America will survive that will be worth fighting to defend."

The increasingly favorable ratings the public gave Mr. Clinton throughout the scandal were a direct affront to conservatives' fervently held conviction that they were "the moral majority." Over the months leading to the president's impeachment and subsequent acquittal by the Senate, only 23 to 28 percent of Americans supported the conservatives' position. In the spring of 1999, the press began to refer to them as the "moral minority." But let's consider their claim. Has our culture become a moral sludge pot, as Weyrich insists? Is there actually some embattled minority that is much more moral than the rest of the country, while the remaining majority is "slouching towards Gomorrah," as former judge Robert Bork puts it?

Nothing could be further from the truth, according to the evidence. Most Americans have grown in the range and intelligence of their moral convictions over the last thirty years. If anything, our moral standards have risen. At the beginning of a new century, most Americans are living in a more complex, nuanced, and mature moral world than ever before. This conclusion takes into account both moral principles and personal relationships, the abstract and the particular, and looks beyond conventional conservative issues like abortion and sexuality to ethical questions in medicine, biotechnology, and the workplace, and to the ethics of destroying rain forests and introducing strange genes into agriculture. Many newspapers and weekly newsmagazines have run articles exploring these issues. In short, the certainties of the past are subjected to almost daily pondering of what is fair and just. As Americans ask new moral questions, we are finding new answers, answers that leave the moral concerns of people like Weyrich and Hyde looking small and pinched. . . .

Clearly, most Americans today have a larger number and a wider variety of moral concerns than ever before.

A Macroview

The Cultural Creatives did not materialize from some eternal cornfield in Iowa, near Kevin Costner's field of dreams. On the contrary, they walked into a scene that was a lot more like Madison Square Garden on the night of a heavyweight brawl. Two powerful subcultures were already contending in the arena, the Moderns and Traditionals. And the fight was, and is, a struggle to define America.

At this point, we'll need to take a cultural macroview and see America through a high-altitude lens. Viewed from up close, this so-called fight of the century could appear to be just another political battle, or a series of individual wrangles over single issues: abortion, school vouchers that allow public money in religious schools, multiculturalism, school prayer, child care, affirmative action and quotas, funding for the arts, gay rights, pornography, the status of women, the meaning of "pro-family," and sex, drugs, and graft in the lives of various politicians. If we view the culture war from too close a perspective, we'll be missing the big picture, because a culture war is not about individual issues and it's not just about politics.

The fight the Cultural Creatives walked in on is basically about who will define our social reality, and whose values will be the official values of our culture. It is a no-holds-barred match over who has the moral authority to decide how Americans live, both in public and in private. As sociologist James Davison Hunter points out in *Culture Wars*, the idea of cultural conflict may sound abstract, but nothing less than a way of life is at stake. And because that conflict is fundamentally a struggle for power, a lot of factors enter in, including "money (a great deal of it), reputation, livelihood, and a considerable array of other resources." When all is said and done, Hunter insists, the culture war is "ultimately about the struggle for domination.". . .

Values Relativism and Values Pluralism

In battle cries that resound through the daily press, Traditional ideologues claim that America has descended into a shallow, permissive period of *values relativism*. This terminology is used by people who are convinced that they have an exclusive claim on the truth, and they apply it to anyone whose values are different from theirs. It says unmistakably, *We live in a homogeneous society, and immoral people are destroying it by watering down and/or polluting the God-given moral absolutes we must all live by.* In the by worst-case scenario, society collapses into an "anything goes" amoral confusion. Many Tradition-

Diverging Paths of the Three Subcultures

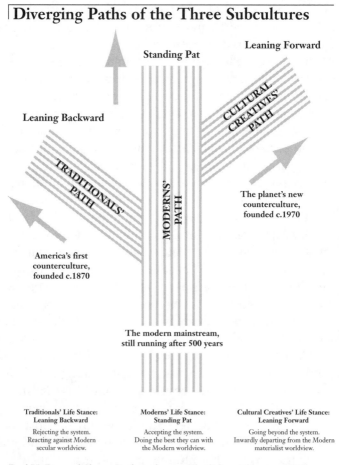

Paul H. Ray and Sherry Ruth Anderson, *The Cultural Creatives*, 2000.

als believe that this is where we are right now.

This belief is not new. The Religious Right has been attacking the values relativism of Moderns for more than two hundred years. George Washington, Thomas Jefferson, Alexander Hamilton, Abraham Lincoln, and Franklin Roosevelt—whoever spoke up for diverse people living side by side with mutual toleration, acceptance, and appreciation of differences was seen as a threat to the moral order. But there's a liberal counterpart term: America has always had a lot more *value pluralism* than Traditionals like to admit. Since *The Federalist Papers*, since Alexis de Tocqueville's *Democracy in America*, and especially since the great immigrations from central and eastern Europe and from Asia, we have long rubbed up against one another's values and moral systems. Contrary to conservative myth, diversity has strengthened American democracy. Exponents of values pluralism, however, go on to say that those on the other side are bigots and idiots.

In fact, both pluralism and relativism are part political philosophy, part myth. Contrary to conservative myth, there was never a time when all Americans agreed on what constitutes proper morality or "who's a good American." And contrary to liberal myth, we haven't been a tossed salad with all the lettuce and tomatoes and sprouts lying happily side by side. Rather, the American heritage has been that we're a fractious, contentious, intolerant, and pluralistic bunch. . . .

The good news is that since the 1960s, most purely religious and ethnic hatreds have relaxed or disappeared entirely. American racism, though still pervasive, is less virulent than in the past and no longer legal. People of goodwill have pretty much had their prayers answered. The bad news is that, since the turmoil of the 1960s, Traditionals of all different stripes have made common cause with one another against the Moderns. Agreeing on a number of issues, they are focusing their fervent opposition against people of their own religion and ethnicity. And Moderns have tended to line up on the other side. . . .

The Moderns

Modern culture originally emerged five hundred years ago in Europe, and over the past three centuries, it has had important roots in the urban merchant classes and the creators of the modern economy, in the rise of the modern state and armies, and in the successes, of scientists, technologists, and intellectuals. It invented our contemporary world, reshaping almost every place on the planet to meet its needs. (What we call Modernism in the arts started in the late nineteenth and early twentieth centuries.) Today's business conservatives tend to idealize 1920s or 1950s images of Modernism, while liberals-to-moderates prefer idealized 1930s and 1960s images. The twentieth-century version encompasses the spectrum of beliefs and politics from big-government liberalism to business conservatism, communism to capitalism, secularism to conventional religion.

The triumph of the Modern world is often celebrated as our liberation from authoritarian political and religious controls. Its great strength is simply in being the dominant culture of the whole planet in our time, able to set agendas, define the terms of discourse, and dominate the mass media. Its great success has been an impressive set of cultural inventions for solving problems that human beings have faced for most of history. It has found ways to:

- diminish toil
- harness the elements
- reduce plagues and illnesses
- create plenty and then distribute it
- house and feed an exploding population
- create effective and productive organizations
- come to terms with increasing social complexity
- build more universal standards of morality and social practices

Modern culture's ambitious agenda was inherited intact from the ancient and early modern worlds. It has solved these problems, often brilliantly. It has gone from village fairs to global market economies, from peasant agriculture to industrial societies, from tiny villages to an urbanized world, from human- and animal-powered handicrafts to a hundred powerful new technologies, from feudalism to nation-states, and from medieval guilds to large-scale corporations. It has brought us noble principles in the realm of political philosophy, which we are now slowly turning into actual political practice: greater equality among persons, personal freedom, justice, civil rights (for example, freedom of speech, religion, and assembly, and fair trials), representative and deliberative democracy, equality before the law. It then uses the principle of universalism to apply those principles to real people and situations. The struggles for civil rights and for women's rights were classic examples of actually living out Modern principles. . . .

The Downside of Modernism

Before the creation of an industrial economy, society lacked the financial means to build and maintain roads, bridges, ports, schools, hospitals, and all the other aspects of a modern infrastructure that we blithely take for granted. Anyone who wanted to launch a new factory could not find workers. Kings and lords couldn't raise armies that would stay through the harvest season. Eventually modernizing elites broke people out of their traditional roles and communities by creating new opportunities, but in doing so they changed far more than the economy. Those who left their communities for the pull of new opportunities often fatally weakened traditional bonds of friendship, religion, class origin, community, and locality.

Once the leave-taking from traditional ways began in earnest, all the king's horses and all the king's men couldn't put them together again. People would occasionally go home to visit their families and old friends, but their children grew up in a different world. Feeling nostalgia was not the same as living the old life, and the looser bonds of the cities, with opportunities winking so invitingly, were too attractive to resist. Perhaps the children forgot what had been nurturing about those bonds in the first place. Or maybe they couldn't imagine how to hold on to both at the same time—the old connections as well as town and city opportunities.

Today's modern achievers, too, often have to tear up their roots in order to succeed. By migrating to another city or state or another country, millions of business travelers are constantly leaving home. One woman executive who travels almost weekly told a *New York Times* reporter, "There are some things that require constant attention. Children, especially. And friendship. That has to constantly be worked on. I no longer make friends, because I'm constantly jerked in and out of my life. Travel's a pain. There's no way around it. . . . Whatever I do, my life feels all turned around, as if I can't focus on what really matters to me."

Where once we were embedded in our communities for life, we now suffer the loss of roots on an epidemic scale. Moderns complain that their relatives and friends are scattered across the continent or across the planet. But at the same time, they want to be sophisticated and up-to-the-minute, not provincial and traditional, which they consider quaint and backward. . . .

The Traditionals

Traditionalism is a culture of memory. Traditionals remember a vanished America and long for its restoration. They place their hopes in the recovery of small-town, religious America, a hazy nostalgic image corresponding to the years from 1890 to 1930. This mythic world was cleaner, more principled, and less conflicted than the one that impinges on us every day today. At that time "men were men," and authority was self-reliant, fixed on the task, and impatient with complexity. Its values are evoked in Jimmy Stewart and John Wayne movies, Fourth of July speeches, and Veterans' Day parades. Often this imagined world never really was.

In smaller cities and towns today, these images are kept alive in stable friendship networks and in communities that still work. A lot more mutual aid is available to Traditionals than to the more mobile Moderns and Cultural Creatives. Even in larger cities, many Traditionals build strong relationships and take care of one another through their religious congregations. Turning away from a daunting modern world they don't like or understand, they turn toward one another to create bulwarks of religious, racial, or ethnic unity against outsiders. Their organizations and congregations give them a sense of strength, safety, and coherence while rejecting or scapegoating those who are judged to be "alien" or "other."

Traditionals hate many of the so-called freedoms of Modernism, like the loosening up of women's roles and the sexual expressiveness and the crazy-quilt inclusiveness for all religions and ethnic origins. . . .

And they remember, or think they do, a time when society had a steady moral compass. A retired factory worker attending a gathering of the all-male evangelical Promise Keepers in 1997 told a reporter, "What I really want to see is all our leaders—the White House—get on their knees and pray for our country. This country was supposedly founded on the Bible," he said. "It's kind of gotten away from it, I feel." Another man at the same gathering, a shipping clerk from Illinois, agreed. "I want to see our nation restored, see us get back to God," he said. "If everybody got back to God, I'm sure crime would fall, racial prejudice would cease, the conflict between the sexes would cease, and abortion would be done away with, just name it. I just feel these things can happen.". . .

The strengths and weaknesses of Traditionalism are two sides of the same coin. Its political strength lies in its enunciation of shared beliefs, principles, and values that can claim a divine sanction, its use of simple images that appeal to less educated people, and its nostalgic appeal to tradition. Its weaknesses are an ethnic and racial politics that, with nostalgia and scapegoating, lends itself to authoritarianism, and its use of a biblical moral framework for every new event, which can make the complex realities of today's world even harder to deal with.

America's First Counterculture

Traditionals were the first counterculture to defect from Modernism. They were already "leaning back" before the American Revolution. Their yearning for a simpler, more moral pasttime appeared as early as the Great Awakening, in the revivalist movements under Jonathan Edwards in colonial Massachusetts. After the Civil War, the counterculture of Traditionalism took root as poor southern whites resisted Reconstruction with Jim Crow codes and the Ku Klux Klan.

Led by rural and small-town Protestant fundamentalist movements for personal salvation, the new subculture was fed by various protest movements as well. The first protests came from farmers, ranchers, and small-town businesses against the dominance of bankers and merchants in cities.

The next targets were giant corporations, such as the railroads. Later waves of protest were set off by failures of family farms and outrage about boom-and-bust agricultural cycles that benefited big business and ruined many farmers. Defections from Modernism intensified as the nineteenth century came to a close. Many people in America's small towns and countryside hated what was going on in the big industrial cities and saw themselves as the ones who could and would uphold "traditional American ways."

But although the new Traditionalism presented itself as an alternative to "city ways," its people were in fact Moderns who were defecting. They were actually members of a counterculture whose *origins and life assumptions were root and branch part of the worldview of early Modernism. . . .*

The Cultural Creatives

Between the extreme positions of the culture wars lies a third way. It is not simply a neutral center but a distinctive expression. Rather than defending an old way of life, Cultural Creatives are bridging an old way of life and a new one. They seem to be unraveling the threads of old garments and weaving new fabric, cutting original designs and sewing together a new one. Many (though not all) want to carry forward what is valuable from the past and integrate it with what's needed for the future. . . .

Cultural Creatives are sick of the fragmentation of Modernism, and they find the Modern-versus-Traditional culture wars to be just another instance of splitting apart what needs to be healed. (The strong exception is the issue of women's rights, where the Cultural Creatives side adamantly with Moderns.) Many describe the culture war as a deliberate ideological distraction from the serious issues that American society needs to come to grips with: that the planet is in peril with the fastest extinction of species in millions of years; that nuclear weapons are still incredibly dangerous; that pesticides and pollutants are contaminating our food, air, and water; that women and children everywhere are endangered by domestic violence; that poor people still have terrible life chances; that discrimination against minorities is still extensive; that medical costs are spiraling out of control and many people lack health insurance; that mainstream medicine is not responding to holistic health issues; that the official culture is still ignoring or mocking spirituality; and that politicians are fiddling with a hundred irrelevancies while Rome burns.

The Cultural Creatives have emerged to a large extent because these failures of Modernism are so blatant that they call into question the official story that we are supposed to live by. Catholic priest and historian Thomas Berry writes, "It's all a question of story. We are in trouble just now because we do not have a good story. We are in between stories. The old story, the account of how the world came to be and how we fit into it, is no longer effective. Yet we have not learned the new story." The old explanation is no longer effective for many of us, but for the time that we believed it, it provided a meaningful context in which life could function. . . .

Cultural Creatives are looking for ways, not so much to tell a new story—no one can *tell* a story deep and true enough to be useful now—but to evoke a new story, to discover a new way of living for a new time. . . .

The promise of the Cultural Creatives is the promise of developing an integral culture that can bring together the traditional and the modern, the planetary and the local, and inner and outer change. The strength of the Cultural Creatives is that they are the part of the population most likely to carry forward a positive vision of the future. They have already begun imagining and developing alternatives to the urgent problems that confront our world. . . .

Beyond the Culture War

So what position do the Cultural Creatives take in the culture war? They refuse to choose sides. They head off in a third direction that's neither left nor right, neither modern nor traditional. They have been deeply involved in most of the new social movements that have appeared since the 1960s and in a host of other cultural inventions as well. Oppositional political movements have influenced them less than cultural movements that try to educate our desires and change our minds about reality. They want to see the big, inclusive picture, and they want to work with the whole system, with all the players. They regard themselves as synthesizers and healers, not just on the personal level but on the planetary level, too. They keep cutting across social class and racial lines, across ideological lines of liberal and conservative, and across national boundaries, rejecting militarism and exploitation, seeking long-term ecological sanity.

Cultural Creatives are interested in experimenting with what might be called women's nonhierarchical models, including feeling *and* action, the personal *and* the political, in a search for humane ways of social transformation. These are, of course, ideals. Their search, like any other, will cover the gamut of human wisdom and folly, honor and criminality. Their ideals are not a lived reality for all Cultural Creatives. But they are in there pitching, trying to create change that moves the culture far beyond the culture war to a new way of life.

Periodical Bibliography

The following articles have been selected to supplement the diverse views presented in this chapter.

Robert J. Bresler — "The End of the Silly Season," *USA Today Magazine*, November 2001.

Ethan Bronner — "Left and Right Are Crossing Paths," *New York Times*, July 7, 1999.

David Brooks — "The New Upper Class: How Conservatives Won the Culture War, and Lost the Peace," *Weekly Standard*, May 8, 2000.

Don Eberly — "'What Chills Me About the Future,'" *American Outlook*, Fall 1999.

John Fonte — "Why There Is a Culture War," *Policy Review*, December 2000.

Stephen Goode and Christopher Jolma — "Correctness Crack-Up," *Insight*, March 18, 2002.

Hugh Heclo — "Hyperdemocracy," *Wilson Quarterly*, Winter 1999.

Paul Hollander — "The Resilience of the Adversary Culture," *The National Interest*, Summer 2002.

Chris Lehmann — "Operation Infinite Jest: The Return of the Culture Wars," *In These Times*, January 21, 2002.

Martin E. Marty — "Why the Talk of Spirituality Today? Some Partial Answers," *Second Opinion*, May 2001.

John Ortberg — "Do They Know Us by Our Love? The First Casualty of the Culture Wars Is Not Truth," *Christianity Today*, May 19, 1997.

Ramesh Ponnuru — "What We're Not Fighting For: The List Includes Short Skirts, Dancing, and Secularism," *National Review*, November 5, 2001.

Liam Rector — "The Culture Wars in a Time of War," *American Poetry Review*, January/February 2002.

Eric Scigliano — "Naming—and Un-naming—Names," *The Nation*, December 31, 2001.

Alan Wolfe — "The Unappreciated Virtue," *The Responsive Community*, Summer 2001.

Is American Culture in Decline?

Chapter Preface

Several recent studies have concluded that the United States experienced a general increase in crime, divorce, teen pregnancy, and substance abuse during the last four decades of the twentieth century. Although some research suggests that such trends—particularly the rate of violent crime—have begun to abate, conservatives often contend that the overall increase in disturbing social problems over the last half century are warning signs of a degenerating culture. Moreover, some conservatives blame the left-wing social movements of the 1960s for the moral decline that they perceive today.

Conservative writer Michael Barone, for example, believes that the countercultural movement of the 1960s seriously damaged American culture. In his view, the excesses of that decade produced a society lacking in values and moral fiber. "Today liberated America turns out to be a place where it is not very safe to walk down the street, nor very serene to grow up, and not very secure to be married," Barone maintains. "We are freer to use drugs, to abandon our families, to have sex of any kind, to abort unwanted children." The result of such "freedom," he contends, is a widespread moral instability that threatens to destroy American culture from the inside out.

Liberals, on the other hand, generally contend that the changes wrought during the 1960s benefited American culture. Despite the upheavals and violence of the decade, its various political movements resulted in an expansion of civil rights for women, minorities, and other historically oppressed groups. Argues history professor Terry H. Anderson, "in just a few years minorities overturned centuries of legal inferiority and discrimination and obtained their rights guaranteed by the Constitution—an astounding achievement for any society. . . . [Racism] has declined. . . . Attitudes that had been held for centuries have changed considerably, have become more tolerant." The challenges to the status quo during the 1960s actually helped make America more humane, diverse, and democratic, Anderson concludes.

Notable thinkers continue to disagree about whether American culture is in decline. The authors in the following chapter offer further discussion on these topics.

"The past four decades . . . have seen troubling signs of . . . cultural deformation."

America Shows Signs of Moral Decline

John Harmon McElroy

America is experiencing disturbing symptoms of cultural and moral decline, argues John Harmon McElroy in the following viewpoint. In the last four decades of the twentieth century, he maintains, divorce, out-of-wedlock births, abortions, and crime increased while public standards of decency and respect for religious values decreased. Core American tenets—such as the belief that the United States is a great nation and that individuals are responsible for their own well-being—are still relatively strong but show signs of weakening, McElroy contends. While America itself has not declined, its symptoms of moral decay point to the need to strengthen traditional values. McElroy is an emeritus professor of English at the University of Arizona and the author of *American Beliefs: What Keeps a Big Country and a Diverse People United*, from which the following excerpt was taken.

As you read, consider the following questions:
1. According to McElroy, what percentage of Americans were born out of wedlock in 1993?
2. What is problematic about the American emphasis on being tolerant and nonjudgmental, in the author's opinion?
3. According to a 1994 Roper poll cited by the author, what values do four generations of Americans share in common?

Americans believe in improvement, not decline. But should the formative and unifying set of beliefs that has been crucial to America's astonishingly rapid rise to prominence ever become deformed, the United States would surely decline. The past four decades (1960–2000) have seen troubling signs of such cultural deformation.

Symptoms of Moral Decline

In no period of American history before the last forty years have families in every class of American society been so disrupted by marital infidelity and divorce (half of all American marriages now end in divorce), out-of-wedlock pregnancies (in 1963, 6.5 percent of Americans were born out of wedlock; in 1993, 30 percent), abortions (now averaging over one million a year) and new venereal diseases such as AIDS and herpes—the cumulative results of the "revolution" against "middle-class morality" on American campuses in the 1960s called the "counterculture," and the 1973 Supreme Court decision on abortion (*Roe v. Wade*). During these same forty years, federal courts across the land have been busy suppressing prayer in public schools and prohibiting the display of the Ten Commandments in public buildings. There has also been an unprecedented surge of drug abuse, the effects of which are now felt in every city, town, and rural community in America and in every class and age group. Criminal acts of many kinds have also risen to record levels and include such disturbing new features of life in America as killers under the age of twelve, recreational murder, and on-the-job and in-school multiple killings—all of which have necessitated record expenditures of public and private resources on personal security, uniformed police forces, and prison facilities.

The same period has likewise seen a growing disrespect for community standards of decency, reflected in speech patterns, obscenity in film and print media, violent song lyrics, and the burning of the American flag—all justified as nothing more than freedom of expression. And never before have so many Americans in all classes of society depended so heavily on government. (Taxes to support government spending now consume 40 percent of a typical American family's earnings. Put another way, the average American family works about three hours a day for tax collectors.) Still another basic change has occurred in public schooling in America: a shift of emphasis from teaching knowledge and skills to teaching "self-esteem"—making it possible for some students to spend twelve years in the system and emerge functionally illiterate. A rewriting of American history as an uninterrupted tale of oppression and victimization has also occurred during these same forty years; and the idea of "multiculturalism" has entirely displaced America's national culture in the thinking of some Americans.

Since the mid-1960s, the growing reluctance of America's schools and universities to flunk students who are not measuring up to minimum standards of performance is part of a larger trend in American society: an unwillingness to pronounce any conduct as wrong. Americans have been made to feel in the past forty years that being "nonjudgmental" is a kind of higher morality. Tolerance and choice—*no matter what is tolerated or chosen*—have been presented as values that override every other. Sophistication, in the minds of too many Americans, has become a more important consideration than shame.

The Culture Remains Strong

As alarming as these symptoms of cultural decline may seem—and they are certainly alarming—they do not lead to the conclusion that American culture has yet been deformed. For one thing, most of the behavioral trends just cited are coming under increasingly heavy criticism, or have leveled off, or have been reversed. And some American beliefs, such as *Helping Others Helps Yourself* and *God Gave Men The Same Birthrights*, have actually been extended and strengthened since the 1960s. Most important, an overwhelming portion of the adult and young adult population of America still consists of responsible individuals.

For example, the Roper Center of Public Opinion Research in 1994 found that Americans across four generations (persons in their late teens to their late sixties and older) agreed that hard work is the key to getting ahead in America; that broadening opportunities is more important than ensuring equality of income; that big government is the greatest threat to America's future; and that they were generally satisfied with their personal lives. Another national poll, taken in 1997, revealed that regardless of region, race, class, or age, most Americans still believe that "people have the power to shape their own lives, no matter what their circumstances, and that the best solutions are reached when people work together, cooperatively." Specifically in this poll, 83 percent agreed that "the USA is the greatest nation on Earth"; 95 percent that "freedom must be tempered by personal responsibility"; 89 percent that people have a "responsibility to help those less fortunate"; 79 percent that "people who work hard in this nation are likely to succeed"; and 81 percent that "a spiritual or religious belief is essential to a fulfilling life."

Moral Indifference

During the 20th century, America has become a society increasingly hostile or indifferent to concepts like good and bad, moral and immoral, noble and base. Today there is even a debate going on in this country about life and death and whether one is necessarily better than the other. The late Timothy Leary, a leader of the countercultural and drug-legalization movement, got a lot of attention in 1977 when he celebrated and advertised his impending death as "the most fascinating experience in life."

Moral indifference might be irrelevant if it were confined to the fringes of American society. After all, human society has always had its cynics. The problem today is that moral indifference has become the standard of some of this nation's most revered, most powerful institutions. It is no longer confined to the intellectual elite. Rather, it permeates much of mainstream society.

William Bennett, *American Legion Magazine*, November 1999.

Predictions of American decline have been made before and have proven false. And it is encouraging to remember that in the forty years from 1840 to 1880, which included a civil war, American beliefs survived. Cultures are tough. After all, cultural beliefs persist because they are durable.

Americans must nonetheless recognize that many of their beliefs as a people have been weakened in the last four decades, particularly the belief *America Is A Chosen Country*, which now seems to embarrass some Americans. (Had the 1997 poll that found an 83 percent agreement that "the USA is the greatest nation on Earth" been taken in 1957, I suspect the percentage of agreement would have been somewhere above 90.) Other American beliefs which—though still strong—have been somewhat diminished are the religious and moral beliefs *God Created Nature And Human Beings*, *God Created A Law Of Right And Wrong*, and *Doing What Is Right Is Necessary For Happiness*; the social and economic beliefs *Everyone Must Work*, *Society Is A Collection Of Individuals*, *Each Person Is Responsible For His Own Well-Being*, and *Opportunities Must Be Imagined* (as opposed to being provided by the government); the political beliefs *A Majority Decides* and *The Least Government Possible Is Best*; and the belief about human nature *Human Beings Will Abuse Power When They Have It* (whose weakening is suggested by judicial decisions nullifying state laws to limit the number of terms of elected representatives).

The end result of the simultaneous weakening of so many American beliefs has been to alter the dynamics of American culture. To account for how and why these beliefs have been weakened is beyond the scope of this viewpoint, but it is certain that since World War II some principles of American culture have been emphasized to the detriment of others. The principle of freedom, for instance, has been promoted without regard to responsibility; calls for improvement have been made without regard to practicality; and equality has sometimes been demanded with a zeal that ignores differences among individuals. Too often in the last forty years of the twentieth century, it seems, America's cultural history has been set aside in favor of uncompromising ideologies.

As always, America's future depends on the unity of the American people, just as George Washington said it did in his Farewell Address in 1796, three years before his death. And that unity is, as always, mostly a matter of the beliefs that Americans share and act on as a people.

"Even when stacked up against the 'good ol' days,' there are plenty of signs of moral progress."

America Is Not in Moral Decline

David Whitman

Contrary to the claims of some conservatives, moral values in the United States are not declining, contends David Whitman in the following viewpoint. Statistics comparing current values with the behavior of twenty to thirty years ago reveal that Americans today are less likely to drive drunk, abuse drugs, engage in serious cheating, or evade paying taxes. Furthermore, Whitman points out, today's adults and teens are more likely to volunteer, donate to charity, and attend religious services. The perception that the United States is in decline may be due to the fact that most Americans believe that they are more moral than the average person. Whitman is a senior writer for *U.S. News & World Report* and the author of *The Optimism Gap: The I'm OK—They're Not Syndrome and the Myth of American Decline.*

As you read, consider the following questions:

1. According to a poll cited by the author, how much on average did Americans donate to charity in 1996? In 1970?
2. What percentage of Americans pray, according to a 1997 Gallup Poll cited by Whitman?
3. What is the "optimism gap," in Whitman's view?

David Whitman, "More Moral—America's Moral Non-Decline," *New Republic*, February 22, 1999. Copyright © 1999 by The New Republic, Inc. Reproduced by permission.

By the time the Monica Lewinsky scandal erupted, three out of four Americans already believed that moral values had weakened in the past quarter-century. Thanks to Bill Clinton's Oval Office high jinks, the case that moral standards are eroding seems stronger than ever. In his bestseller *The Death of Outrage*, William Bennett argues that the lack of public outcry over the president's adultery and prevarication is but one more sign that people's "commitment to long-standing American ideals has been enervated." Al Gore would disagree with Bennett's analysis of Clinton, but he, too, believes that "there is indeed a spiritual crisis in modern civilization."

Yet, for all the bipartisan hand-wringing about moral decline, there is surprisingly little evidence that Americans act more immorally today than they did a quarter-century ago. In fact, just the opposite seems to be true—as even a few conservatives are beginning to concede. In a 1999 issue of the right-leaning magazine *The American Enterprise*, editor-in-chief Karl Zinsmeister urges fellow conservatives not "to accuse the American people of becoming morally rotten. Especially when there exist abundant data suggesting that the residents of our land are actually becoming less morally rotten." It is still true, of course, that millions of citizens continue to err and sin, and that the culture now has a surfeit of coarseness, from noxious rap lyrics to the *Jerry Springer Show*. But, if one looks beyond the anecdotes, the picture of how people behave is unexpectedly encouraging.

Compared with their predecessors of a quarter century ago, Americans today are less likely to drink to excess, take drugs, rely on the dole, drive drunk, or knowingly evade paying taxes. They give more money to charity and spend as much or more time in church. And they are more likely than their predecessors to do good Samaritan work among the poor, sick, and elderly. Despite fears of random violence, FBI reports suggest that fewer people were murdered by strangers in 1997 (2,067) than in 1977 (about 2,500), even though the U.S. population grew by 47 million during that time. The dramatic drop in the number of Americans victimized by murder, burglary, and theft represents another well-known illustration of moral progress, but there are many more.

Charity and Religion

For example, Americans now donate significantly more money to charity than they did a generation ago, as Everett Carll Ladd, director of the Roper Center for Public Opinion Research, documents in a forthcoming book. Adjusted for inflation, Americans gave about $525 per adult to charity in 1996. That is 50 percent more than Americans on average donated in 1970 ($349) and roughly triple what people gave in 1950 ($179). Starting in 1977, pollsters also began regularly asking adults whether they were involved in charity or social services, such as helping the poor, the sick, or the elderly. The ranks of those participating roughly doubled from 26 percent in 1977 to 54 percent in 1995. Volunteer work by college students is up, too. In 1998, 74 percent of college freshmen had done volunteer work the preceding year, the highest such figure since researchers started tracking it in 1984.

Charity has often gone hand in hand with religion, so perhaps it is not surprising to learn that religious faith, too, is not in decline. On the contrary, America remains a deeply religious nation, with a reinvigorated evangelical movement. In 1997, the Gallup Poll replicated one of its earliest surveys on Americans' religious practices from 1947. The 50-year update found that the same percentage of Americans pray (90 percent), believe in God (96 percent), and attend church once a week. One of the few differences between the two eras was that Americans were actually more likely to give grace or give thanks aloud in 1997 than in 1947 (63 percent compared with 43 percent).

Both adults and teens are now as likely to belong to a church or synagogue as their counterparts were 25 years ago, and they attend religious services a bit more often. In December 1998, 42 percent of adults reported attending a service at a church or synagogue the previous week—a tad higher than the 40 percent or so who said they had attended services in 1972, 1950, and 1940. As the political scientist Seymour Martin Lipset writes in his book *American Exceptionalism*, "Religious affiliation and belief in America are much higher in the twentieth century than in the nineteenth, and have not decreased in the post–World War II era."

Serious Cheating Is Down

While everyone "knows" that cheating on tests has exploded in recent decades, the few studies that have looked at trends over time suggest a different picture. A 1996 analysis by Donald McCabe and Linda Klebe Trevino of Rutgers University at nine state universities did find that cheating on tests and exams increased significantly from 1963 to 1993. But serious cheating on written work, such as plagiarism and turning in work done by others, had declined slightly, leading the researchers to conclude that "the dramatic upsurge in cheating heralded by the media was not found."

Cheating on taxes also appears to be no worse than in the recent past. Since 1973, the Internal Revenue Service has tracked the "voluntary compliance rate," a figure used to describe the percentage of total tax liability that individuals and corporations pay voluntarily. In 1992, the voluntary compliance rate for the individual income tax was roughly 83 percent, a hair higher than in 1973.

A Drop in Drug Use

As for another vice—drug use—Americans seem to be doing better, not worse. Use of illicit drugs peaked in 1979, when 14.1 percent of the population reported having used an illicit drug the previous month, more than double the 1997 figure of 6.4 percent. Cocaine use peaked in 1985; Americans were four times as likely to use cocaine then as they are today. The trends are similar among high school seniors (though marijuana use has risen since 1992).

At the same time, heavy alcohol consumption, binge drinking, and drunken driving have all declined. Heavy alcohol use—defined as having five or more drinks on the same occasion on each of five or more days in the previous month—is at its lowest point since 1985, when the federal government first started tracking the figure. In 1985, 8.3 percent of the population were heavy drinkers compared with 5.4 percent in 1997, a drop of about a third. The decline in drunken driving has been equally marked. In 1997, the number of people killed in alcohol-related crashes dropped to less than 40 percent of all traffic fatalities for the first time since the government started tracking this statistic in 1975. Americans consumed about as much alcohol per person in 1995 as in 1945—and drank substantially less than in 1970.

Less Political Corruption

For all the talk of scandal, and despite the official statistics, political corruption seems to be waning, too. In 1996, 952 individuals were indicted in federal prosecutions for public corruption, more than triple the number in 1975. Yet most historians believe the apparent rise in corruption stems from the proliferation of special prosecutors and inspector generals, not from a real upsurge in unethical conduct. New disclosure rules, government intercessions in allegedly corrupt unions, a law enforcement crackdown on the mob, the disappearance of Tammany Hall–style urban political machines and "good-time Charlie" governors, and a more watchful press all seem to have reduced bribes, hush money, and other blatant types of political corruption. Even William Bennett concedes in *The Death of Outrage* that "in general, politics today is less corrupt than perhaps at any point in American history."

America Is Not Falling Apart

America is [not] falling apart. On the one hand, the institutional structure of the United States has the capacity to diffuse potentially divisive conflicts between classes, religious sects, and ethnic communities throughout society—rather than concentrating them against the state. On the other hand, as long as the economy is healthy, putative new identities and groups do not offer any real challenge to the basic premises of American culture, nor is the highly flexible social fabric of America likely to be torn asunder by their demands. Whether black or white, gay or straight, female or male, the vast majority of Americans continue to believe in the possibilities of economic success and to act as if the world was made up of nice, nonjudgmental individuals, who build familial communities through mutual and voluntary cooperation. Despite the inevitable and wrenching tensions and paradoxes implicit in this idealized belief system, it shows no signs of losing its hold.

Charles Lindholm and John A. Hall, *Daedalus*, Spring 1997.

Granted, not all the news on the moral front is good. One institution that undeniably weakened in the past quarter-century is the family. Since the early '70s, out-of-wedlock childbearing has skyrocketed. Child abuse and neglect have risen, too—thanks mainly to the advent of crack—and most noncustodial parents still don't pay their child support.

Yet other much-lamented changes in family life do not really demonstrate a rise (or fall) in collective virtue. The surge in divorce suggests that Americans now lack a sense of commitment, but most divorced couples do not think they are acting immorally—more often, they think they have done the right thing by ending a troubled marriage. Many couples similarly defend cohabitation, once deemed to be "living in sin," as a sensible trial run at marriage.

Signs of Progress

Some moral behavior that has improved in the past quarter-century, particularly the reduction in criminality and drug-taking, is still worse today than it was in the 1950s. But, even when stacked up against the "good ol' days," there are plenty of signs of moral progress. In the 1950s, well over half of the nation's black population lived under almost apartheid-like conditions through much of the South. Millions of women faced sexual discrimination and were denied the right to pursue a calling of their own. Society treated the elderly shabbily, with more than one in three living in poverty (compared with one in ten today). The disabled faced blatant, ugly bigotry, as did homosexuals.

Why hasn't the news about moral progress reached the public? In part, the reason is that it is often thought that people were more moral in earlier eras. Back in 1939, a Gallup Poll showed that 62 percent of the population believed that Americans were happier and more contented in the horse-and-buggy days; a survey taken by Elmo Roper two years earlier found that half of the population felt religion was then losing its influence on American life as well.

But part of the explanation for the public disbelief is that Americans experience an "optimism gap." When members of the public voice distress about family breakdown they are almost always referring to other people's families. Yet the vast majority of citizens do not have serious moral qualms about themselves or their families. Surveys show that most people think they are more moral than the average American, and members of the public repeatedly describe their own families as happy ones with strong ties.

In 1997, *U.S. News & World Report* conducted a revealing survey of 1,000 adults who were asked to rate the chances that various celebrities would one day get into heaven. Topping the list of famous people bound for heaven was Mother Teresa, who had not yet died. Nearly 80 percent of those polled thought it likely that the Nobel Peace Prize winner would one day get her wings. But the survey's most startling finding was that the individuals voted most likely to get into heaven were, well, those being polled. Eighty-seven percent felt that they were heaven-bound, compared with 79 percent who thought the same of Mother Teresa.

Most Americans, in short, hold a generous opinion of their own morals, even while they remain acutely aware of others' failings. But, if Americans can convince themselves that they are bound for heaven, it may also be time to acknowledge that the rest of the nation is not making a beeline for purgatory.

"Hollywood is an integral part of the process of supplanting individualism with a planned society and the old morality with a new amoral order."

Popular Culture Is Contributing to America's Decline

Jennifer A. Gritt

In the following viewpoint, Jennifer A. Gritt contends that the mainstream media and entertainment industry are undermining America's founding principles of individualism and religious faith. Hollywood producers and directors are consciously working to subvert the nation's traditional values by making movies containing profanity, violence, drug use, explicit sex, and anti-Christian messages, Gritt maintains. By producing such mindless and crude entertainment, Hollywood and other promoters of popular culture hope to manipulate the population—especially youth—into accepting amoral and socialist solutions to America's problems. Gritt is an editorial assistant for the *New American*, a conservative biweekly journal.

As you read, consider the following questions:
1. According to Gritt, what is the truth about the artists who were blacklisted from working in Hollywood during the 1940s and 1950s?
2. In the author's opinion, how is drug usage usually depicted in popular movies?
3. How do Hollywood films typically portray Christianity, according to Gritt?

On October 27, 1997, Hollywood celebrities gathered at the Motion Picture Academy of Arts and Sciences in Beverly Hills to see the production *Hollywood Remembers the Blacklist*. Replete with dramatic narration, compelling photos, live skits, and witness testimony, Hollywood paid tribute to the "victims" of the blacklist. The entertainment industry's decision to not hire anyone determined to be a Communist or Communist sympathizer during what has been historically labeled the "Red Scare" was vilified as an assault on freedom of thought and expression.

Of the many called to testify before the House Committee on Un-American Activities, eight screenwriters, a director, and a producer openly defied the proceedings. All were members of the Communist Party and their refusal to cooperate made them famous as the "Hollywood Ten." Marsha Hunt, one of the stars who flew to Washington in 1947 to support Hollywood's accused, explained to the audience: "We were flying to keep the First Amendment alive." She went on to proclaim, "As the virus [fear of Communism] spread across the nation, for a decade, this was no longer the land of the free, nor the home of the brave." Her conclusion was met with fervent applause.

But as Kenneth Lloyd Billingsley documents in his book *Hollywood Party*, the virus infecting Hollywood was not "fear of Communism" but Communism itself. And that virus was not merely the product of Communist ideology but of Communist organization. As Billingsley explains: "Everything that Party writers produced had to be vetted by Party officials. Rarely if ever did a first draft of a play, novel, or article run as the author had first composed it." Elia Kazan, a former Communist Party member who won an Oscar for *On the Waterfront*, recalled that "the most dangerous thing the Party had to cope with [was] people thinking for themselves."

The Real Blacklisting

Why would a *government* committee be worried about Communist infiltration of Hollywood? How much of an impact could actors, producers, and screenwriters *really* have on America? Hollywood's night of remembrance fell short of answering questions such as these. It chose to ignore the ramifications of Communist influence on American culture and glorified supposed "victims" of the blacklist when in fact the majority of those blacklisted *were* either members of the Communist Party or were active in Communist fronts. Two-time vice-presidential candidate and former Communist leader Ben Gitlow clearly understood Moscow's agenda: "We were volunteer members of a militarized colonial service, pledged to carry out the decisions of our supreme rulers resident at Moscow anywhere in the world but particularly in the land we were colonizing for Communism, the United States." And that colonizing continued. Many of the blacklisted Communists continued to work in Hollywood under pseudonyms, and by the 1960s most had been welcomed back openly, as heroes. The *real* blacklisting was carried out against the anti-Communists, such as Elia Kazan, Edward Dmytryk, Adolphe Menjou, Morrie Ryskind, and Richard Macaulay, all highly successful artists whose careers were ruined because they opposed the Communist exploitation of the silver screen.

But Communism is dead, right? Not according to Balint Vazsonyi, who experienced not only Communism but another variant of the total state, Nazism, in his native Hungary prior to emigrating to America. In his book *America's 30 Years War*, Vazsonyi warns: "For the past thirty years, all aspects of our lives—and all of our institutions—have been moving in one direction: away from America's founding principles. . . . And every time we move away from [them], we move in the direction of the sole realistic alternative." He points out that totalitarian socialism, or what he refers to as "The Idea," has gone through "countless transformations and as many versions. It has been 'Bolshevism' in Russia, 'Fascism' in Italy, 'National Socialism' in Germany, 'Democratic Socialism' in Sweden, and the 'Long March' and 'Cultural Revolution' in China."

The Bolsheviks were able to come to power through a violent and bloody revolution that was facilitated by the fact that the Russian people did not possess a long heritage of freedom that other Westerners possessed. The Nazis, on the other hand, had to proceed much more gradually in converting democratic Germany into a police state. And such is the case in the United States, where the architects of the total state have had to proceed incrementally, employing a [socialist] strategy to take control of our cultural institutions. Vazsonyi elaborates: "The Idea has been successfully installed in America's schools, as well as in most of the information and entertainment media. Academia, Hollywood, the news media, the National Education Association, and the environmental movement are far more effective [at promoting totalitarian socialism] than any political party. And, as high school textbooks, college courses, television newscasts, or national newspapers attest, the purpose is the *transformation* of America."

Hollywood's Role

Hollywood is an integral part of the process of supplanting individualism with a planned society and the old morality with a new amoral order. Consider, for example, the explosion of homosexual/lesbian characters and themes appearing in television programs and movies in recent years. Is this Hollywood responding to the demands of average Americans or an attempt by moviemakers to reflect the "real" face of society? Hardly. It is a triumph of Hollywood's "Velvet Mafia," the cinematic demimonde led by the likes of billionaire homosexual activist David Geffen of SKG DreamWorks. Geffen (the "G" in SKG DreamWorks, with Steven Spielberg and Jeffrey Katzenberg) was the guiding light behind SKG's *American Beauty*, the perverse 1999 homoagitprop film that won five Oscars. Bruce Cohen, the homosexual co-producer of *American Beauty*, explained the exciting possibilities this presented: "The excitement about mainstream films is the chance to get these messages across subtly in films that mainstream America is going to see. We have definitely hit a segment of the audience that is not used to seeing gay and lesbian characters."

One of television's most celebrated producer/directors is Steven Bochco, the force behind such Emmy-acclaimed shows as *Hill Street Blues*, *NYPD Blue*, and *Murder One*. Bochco has repeatedly stated his subversive intent, declaring that his creations aim at destroying *all* television taboos concerning profanity, blasphemy, nudity, homosexuality, explicit sexual content, incest—virtually everything. And he and his fellow culture vultures have done exactly that.

TV and movie mogul Ted Turner, infamous for his malicious attacks on Christianity, opined in 1999 that the Ten Commandments, are "a little out of date." "If you're only going to have 10 rules," said the vice chairman of Time Warner, "I don't know if adultery should be one of them."

Undermining Authority

What must be acknowledged is that many of the most corrupting viruses are now being borne along . . . by an entertainment and information media culture, and that this omnipresent culture is displacing the core social institutions that once shaped and molded the democratic citizen. Whereas parents, priests, and pedagogues once presided over the socialization of the young, now television, film, music, cyberspace, and the celebrity culture of sports and entertainment dominate this process of shaping youthful attitudes and beliefs. It is popular mass culture that largely informs our most basic understanding of society, our public life, our obligations to each other, and even the nature of the American experiment. . . .

Much of what passes for culture today is, in fact, anti-culture. Its chief aim is to emancipate, not restrain; to give free reign to human appetite, not moderate it. The role of entertainment, we are frequently told by entertainers themselves, is to challenge and stretch standards. "Break the rules!" "Have no fear!" "Be yourself!" are the common themes within mainstream cultural programming, and they are designed to discredit traditional forms of authority.

Don Eberty, *American Outlook*, Fall 1999.

Responding to the howls of protest by parents against the torrents of toxic waste spewing from Hollywood, the cultural polluters repeatedly insist that they are "sensitive" to these concerns and will police themselves. Dr. Ted Baehr, founder of the Christian Film and Television Commission and publisher of *Movieguide*, doesn't buy it. "The new television rating system is truly a sham," says Baehr. "Jack Valenti [president of the Motion Picture Association of America] knows that ratings give license to the industry to do as they please, for as long as there is a rating on it, the industry feels free of their moral responsibility."

Dr. Baehr points to numerous self-indicting statements by movie industry leaders, like those above by Turner and Cohen, and this lame concession by NBC's president of entertainment, Scott Sassa: "In some cases, we could use a few more words between 'Hello' and 'Would you sleep with me?'" That kind of insulting response shows "sensitivity" to the legitimate concerns of parents and those concerned about our descent into the sewer. "This is just an example of how so many of these Hollywood elites are totally out of touch and morally rudderless," Dr. Baehr says.

Sex, Drugs, and God

Relentless glorification of the drug culture is one of the tools used in Hollywood's demolition of society. Drug usage is commonly portrayed either as a practical escape from reality, or as a casual everyday behavior. Or worse, it is depicted as a badge of "hipness."

"Classic" films like Quentin Tarantino's *Pulp Fiction*, which is famous for its dance scene where an equally stoned John Travolta and Uma Thurman win a contest at a disco-restaurant, are marketed to youths. Likewise, *Trainspotting*, the story of a partially reformed drug addict dealing with the drudgery of life, carefully intertwines drug usage with hipness. In the underground club scene, Ecstasy is the drug of choice and is duly promoted by star Holly Hunter in *Living Out Loud*, a film about a lonely divorcée coping with the end of her marriage.

As evidenced by the Rockdale County, Georgia, sex debacle [a syphilis outbreak that occurred among Rockdale teenagers in 1996], today's teenagers are unaware of the consequences that result from sexual promiscuity. Ignoring the possibilities of pregnancy and disease, today's media-drenched teens have been conditioned to believe that satisfying every hormonal impulse is something that is as normal as it is fun. Where are they getting this message? High school cult favorites such as *American Pie*, *Wild Things*, *Cruel Intentions*, and *Chasing Amy* boast plots completely built around indiscriminate teenage carnality. HBO's hit show *Sex and the City* not only promotes promiscuity, but the notion that marriage is passé.

The oil and water mixture of Hollywood and religion results in a programmed assault on traditional values. Religious faith, if depicted at all, is usually illustrated through unappealing Christian characters whose aggressive spiritual expression appears fanatical to a media-conditioned audience that is becoming increasingly hostile to organized faith. Religious believers are often portrayed as closed-minded, intolerant, ultra-conservative reactionaries. *Dogma*, one of the recent attacks on the Catholic Church, poses as a story of two angels (Matt Damon and Ben Affleck) trying to get back into heaven. Complete with heavy profanity, violent killings, in-line skating teenagers as the devil's henchmen, and rock singer Alanis Morissette as "God," the movie is an endless display of ridicule for the sanctity of the Catholic religion. The film ends with Ben Affleck thanking God for allowing him to die because he could no longer stand life on earth.

Hollywood's remorseless depiction of Christianity as a religion of extreme right-wing, racist bigots, or as the comedic leftover of a sentimental era that can no longer provide the answers to a humanist society, does more than just insult a great portion of the American people. It seeks to destroy the spiritual base of the republic bequeathed us by our Founding Fathers and strip our culture of all reference to Jesus Christ, whom Christians recognize as God and Savior, and whom even many non-Christians can look to as one of humankind's greatest teachers of what is right and wrong.

Embracing the Fog

"Generation X," the media-created term used to classify teens and twenty-somethings of the 1990s, came to epitomize the grunge culture that saturated the music and entertainment industries. Alternative rock bands such as Nine Inch Nails, Nirvana, Pearl Jam, and the Red Hot Chili Peppers provided the background music for the cultural drama of young Americans destined to aimlessly walk the earth wearing oversized, earth-toned pants, and long, baggy shirts. Lost, disillusioned, nihilistic—this new breed of slackers was supposedly only concerned with finding new and exciting ways to express their anger at their world, their lives, and especially their parents. Because they were lost in a sea of hero-less violence and psychological distress, Gen Xers were said to hold particular contempt for baby boomers and their "work hard, you'll succeed" attitude.

However, these descriptions, endlessly repeated and promoted by MTV and its mimics in the major media, were really self-fulfilling promotions for youthful decadence. In a late attempt to acknowledge some resistance to the entrenched stereotyping of some 38 million young Americans, the June 6, 1994 issue of *Newsweek* revealed that polls have determined that 1 in 10 twenty-somethings rejected the notion that "Generation X" even existed, and that "69 percent believed that 'people get ahead by their own hard work'"—much to the dismay of those seeking to propagate a nihilistic youth culture. The media-favored term quickly faded from use.

Enter Generation Y. A new media attempt is underway to shape and develop the next generation of youth. Born with their fingers attached to a keyboard, this cyber-generation eats, sleeps, and breathes on the World Wide Web. Unfortunate products of socialist-designed "dumbing down" programs, when these teens aren't busy surfing the Net, they're out there proving to the world how intellectually challenged they are. Gen Y is packaged as constantly searching for the next distraction—the more fun and exciting, the better. At the 2000 MTV Movie Awards, Generation Y voted for not only their favorite movies, but for categories that included best action sequence, best villain, best fight scene, and best kiss. According to the July/August 2000 issue of *Film Comment*, "MTV is nothing if not trendy." With role models like "teen America's favorite girlfriend" Cameron Diaz announcing to a camera that she has to pee, it is no wonder that *Film Comment* writer Alissa Quart reported: "Gen Y's teens like their actors to seem fun, dumb, and at ease—in other words, like *regular* teens." (Emphasis added.) With the film industry aggressively marketing R-rated films to teenagers, it is apparent that not only is Hollywood largely determining who teens are, they're claiming to know what they want.

Hollywood vs. Reality

With approximately 70 percent of films being produced carrying an "R" rating and a number of those targeting underage youth, the Motion Picture Association of America recently came under attack by the Federal Trade Commission. Denouncing the entertainment industry's tactics of marketing violent and sexually explicit material to teenagers, the FTC called for greater self-regulation and better enforcement at the box office. MPAA head Jack Valenti reacted defiantly to the FTC scolding. According to the Associated Press, Valenti declared: "If we are causing moral decay in this country, we ought to have an explosion of crime." He defended the industry's mass production of explicit material as necessary in order to generate profits and congratulated its self-policing effort to card underage teenagers attempting to purchase R-rated movie tickets. "For almost 32 years," Valenti emphasized, "this industry has been the only segment of our national marketplace that voluntarily turns away revenues at the box office. . . ."

However, even if box office enforcement were effective at not selling R-rated movie tickets to underage teens, there is virtually nothing to prevent teens from sneaking into their film of choice after they have entered the theater complex. Furthermore, Valenti's claim that the film industry turns away revenue at the box office does not coincide with the fact that the 19 top-grossing movies of all time have been rated PG-13 or lower. If money is the determining factor, why wouldn't Hollywood produce less explicit, more family oriented material? Could it be that the real motivation behind the unrelenting mass-production of R-rated films is the conscious demolition and transformation of American society?

Hollywood appears unwilling to change its program of subjecting the American public to greater amounts of sex, drugs, and violence—falsely claiming that this is what America wants. But Hollywood's output is not a true reflection of America's moral climate; it is a reflection of what the cultural subverters hope America will become. Today's youth, especially, are facing an immense struggle against an industry seeking to define, manipulate and condition them with explicit images of depravity, hopelessness, and mindless diversion—with the grand design that younger generations will eventually be manipulated into accepting socialist remedies.

4

"The same social changes we are seeing in real life—reconnecting with family, regaining respect for institutions and community, fleeing the rat race—[are] already rampant in books, in movies, and especially on TV."

Popular Culture Reveals America's Strengths

Part I: Jeanne McDowell and Andrea Sachs;
Part II: Geneva Overholser

The authors of the following two-part viewpoint maintain that much of contemporary popular culture showcases America's strengths rather than its weaknesses. In Part I, *Time* journalists Jeanne McDowell and Andrea Sachs discuss how recent books, movies, and television series feature characters who value home, family, and community with a focus on such topics as sacrifice, family reconciliation, and the emptiness of materialism. In Part II, *Washington Post* columnist Geneva Overholser contends that America's popular culture should be judged by its finest—not its worst—representatives.

As you read, consider the following questions:

1. What is the subject of the films *Life as a House* and *The Royal Tenenbaums*, according to McDowell and Sachs?
2. In the opinion of McDowell and Sachs, what prompted the popularity of the "money-isn't-everything" theme in current movies and television shows?

I

Over the past months [at the end of 2001], it has become tempting—and too easy—to mark Sept. 11 [2001, when terrorists flew planes into the World Trade Center and the Pentagon] as the day life turned bad and we turned good. The Great Before, goes the myth, was a time of peace, plenty and triviality, when we coasted in blissful self-absorption, drunk on day trading, egged on by a selfish, amoral popular culture. The period has become as instantly stereotyped as the '60s: just replace acid with half-caf lattes, Charles Manson with Gary Condit, and Woodstock with *Survivor*. It's a response that is both self-loathing (smacking of the Falwellian idea that we somehow brought disaster on our frivolous selves) and comforting (if so much was taken from us, shouldn't we get a sense of moral superiority in return?). It's also, in one important way, wrong. Of course our collective near-death experience changed many of us. But if our popular artists know anything about us, we were ready to change long before.

Consider: An elderly woman tries to reunite her dysfunctional family for Christmas. Successful urbanites quit their stressful jobs and stream back to their hometowns. A generation of ordinary young folk are called on to risk their lives for their country. These are not examples from a social-trend story about our world after Sept. 11 but the subjects of some of the most popular entertainments created before. The same social changes we are seeing in real life—reconnecting with family, regaining respect for institutions and community, fleeing the rat race—were already rampant in books, in movies and especially on TV, to an extent that suggests the real-world longing for change may be deep-seated enough to last. When it comes to changed priorities and renewed purpose, popular culture has been there, done that and bought the bowling alley.

That bowling alley is the setting of TV's *Ed*, in which a New York City lawyer quits his high-powered firm to move home to Stuckeyville, Ohio, woo his high school crush and buy the local Stuckeybowl lanes. Today half the stressed-out skyscraper workers in Manhattan have a comparable escape fantasy, but *Ed* and its newly resonant theme of fleeing to the past debuted more than a year ago [in 2000]. And we have seen similar homecoming stories on *Providence* (L.A. plastic surgeon moves home, works in clinic), *Judging Amy* (big-city lawyer moves home, becomes a judge) and . . . *Crossing Jordan* (medical examiner moves home, solves crimes with Dad), to name a few.

Nostalgia shows like *The Wonder Years* appealed to adults by re-creating their childhood past. But this gaggle of series offers the greater, reassuring fantasy that you can re-create your childhood today, right down to, as on Ellen DeGeneres' *The Ellen Show*, moving back into your old bedroom. "The characters experience a new beginning but also have an anchor and things that are familiar to them," says *Ed* creator Rob Burnett. "There is a certain feeling of trying to recapture youth that we find appealing."

And many characters are not just recapturing their childhoods but resolving them. Even before the terrorist attacks moved families to enter counseling, artists were rejecting the easy, cynical contemporary assumption that estrangement from your family is as much a rite of adulthood as buying your first legal beer. Take Jonathan Franzen's best-selling novel *The Corrections*, a multigenerational saga about—remarkably, for an erudite postmodernist who dissed Oprah's Book Club—the wholly Oprah-esque topic of family reconciliation: three neurotic, grown children are reunited by their traditionalist mother, Enid, for one last Christmas before their father succumbs to Parkinson's dementia. Two major fall [2001] movies, *Life as a House* and . . . *The Royal Tenenbaums*, likewise involve parents facing death and trying to set things right with their families. Suddenly, the notions of family and connection seem a little less unhip and middlebrow. "The community is a palpable reality at a time of crisis," says novelist Joyce Carol Oates. "People need their friends, they need one another, and they need their families."

Pop culture's families have hardly become idyllic again; there's just a greater sense that they are worth the effort to salvage them. The WB's teen soap *Dawson's Creek*, which became a hit in 1997, was a prime example of pop culture's dysfunction assumption. The show's parents, when they were not absent altogether, were cold, abusive, philandering or in jail. The teen-friendly message: All your problems really are your parents' fault. But this [2001] season has seen the lead character dealing seriously with his father's death in an accident, and last season [of 2000] the same youth-oriented network debuted *Gilmore Girls*, in which a single mom renews her strained relationship with her parents after 16 years. Even ABC's slick new spy thriller *Alias* centers on a young double agent trying to reconcile with her dad, also a double agent, and come to terms with his personal duplicities. "To me, it is the most important story in the show," says creator J.J. Abrams—all the more so after Sept. 11. "Sometimes it takes a traumatic event to reprioritize and understand that some differences aren't worth holding a grudge over."

Thinking about doing community work, getting involved, quitting that all-consuming job? Again, pop culture got there first. [In 2000] the holiday hit *Cast Away* tore Tom Hanks from his hard-charging career as a FedEx manager by stranding him on an island, and Kevin Spacey's *Pay It Forward* preached the gospel of philanthropy. (In fact, with 1999's satire of suburban materialism *American Beauty* and [2001's] carpe-diem *K-PAX*, Spacey has made a kind of millennial change-thy-life trilogy.) The most popular new TV drama [in the fall of 2001] *The Guardian*, features a cynical corporate attorney who finds purpose doing community service as a children's lawyer.

This money-isn't-everything vogue probably originated as a backlash against the long boom years of the '90s. (Conveniently, Americans, real and fictional, tend to start rethinking the fast track just when the economy stops paying off like a rigged slot machine. The early-'90s recession saw downsized professionals pursuing the simple life and a New York City doctor finding quirky meaning in Alaska on *Northern Exposure*.) But this backlash isn't about just money. It's about a general cultural exhaustion, about moving from post-Vietnam mistrust of institutions (*The X-Files*) to respect for them (*The West Wing*), from surrogate families (*Seinfeld*) to flawed but richly explored ones (*The Sopranos*). Above all, it is about rediscovering community in a culture that lionized the individual. Even the dark drama *Six Feet Under* features a gay character finding solace in, of all uncool places, his church. Most conspicuous is the World War II mania, from *Saving Private Ryan* and Tom Brokaw's encomium *The Greatest Generation* right up to [the] HBO miniseries *Band of Brothers*, which has rolled boomer reconnection with parents, guilt over easy prosperity and a longing for communal purpose (be careful what you wish for) all into one trendlet.

And yet, as much as all these works anticipated the changes that would come after Sept. 11, in a way Sept. 11 changed them too. *Band of Brothers* debuted on Sept. 9. Two days and 5,000 lives later, its tag line about ordinary people in extraordinary times was no longer a mere historical reference. On its release, the jacket art of *The Corrections*—a clean-cut family sitting at a holiday table laden with turkey, cranberry-jelly slices and radish rosettes—seemed like a Lynchian dig at Norman Rockwell Americana. Today the image just seems, well, nice. And before Sept. 11 a literate reader would most likely have identified with the novel's neurotic, sophisticated grown children. Today it's hard for even the most jaded not to feel more like Enid, hoping against hope and reality for one more normal holiday.

II

Loathing the culture is as American as apple pie. We loathe it from the right, decrying rents in our moral and social fabric, and yearning for traditions lost. We loathe it from the left, bemoaning the distorting grip of capitalism and yearning for more government funding.

Even when good news pierces the gloom, we hasten to assert that socially and culturally we're still headed for hell in a handbasket. Take a 1999 piece in the *National Journal* called "This Perplexing Union":

"On the eve of a new century, there is no escaping the good news," it says, reciting some of it. But don't get too cheery: "Much of our popular culture is garbage, celebrity is almost infinitely more valued than achievement, there is little stigma to greed and materialism."

In 1998 the culture ministers of 19 nations, including America's best friends, met in Ottawa, Canada, to ponder how to protect themselves and their culture from—well, from us.

We weren't invited.

Moral Rot?

So how exactly does it look these days, this culture found by many to be so offensive, this "moral rot" that some smell upon us? Let us check a few indices of moral and cultural health, starting with young people.

After two decades of increase, the proportion of high school students who have had sex has fallen 11 percent in the 1990s, according to a federal report released in 1998. For the first time in the 1990s, fewer than half the teenagers surveyed reported having sex; among boys, the decline was striking—49 percent, versus 57 percent in 1991. Teenage births and abortions are both down.

A Vital Popular Culture

New musical genres continue to blossom. The twentieth century has seen the development of blues, soul, rhythm and blues, jazz, ragtime, swing, rock, country and western, rap, and bluegrass, as well as more recent forms of electronic music. Some of the most significant modern artists are still around, playing and recording for our enjoyment. We can hear Bob Dylan and the Rolling Stones in concert, still in good form, even if not at their youthful peak.

Film is the art of the 20th century, par excellence. It combines drama, music, and high technology to entertain and inspire large audiences. Moviegoers all around the world want to see American films. Some movie buffs complain that "they don't make 'em like they used to," but the best American films of the last 20 years—my list would include *The Thin Blue Line*, *Blue Velvet*, *Basic Instinct*, *Schindler's List*, *Dangerous Liaisons*, *L.A. Confidential*, *Titanic*, and *The Truman Show*—belie that opinion. (The viewer who disagrees with my list will have no trouble coming up with his or her own favorites.) Art movies and independent films show continued vitality.

Tyler Cowen, *CATO Policy Report*, September/October 1998.

Or take alcohol. In 1980, 72 percent of high school seniors said they had consumed alcohol recently. In 1996, that figure was 51 percent. In 1985, 17 percent of students said they had tried cocaine. In 1996, it was 7 percent.

Violent crime is at its lowest point in 25 years. Since the early 1990s, homicides are down about 20 percent.

As for cultural indicators, a 1998 Cato Institute report called "Is Our Culture in Decline?" cited some dramatic statistics. The average American buys more than twice as many books today as in 1947. Bookstores jumped nearly tenfold in that time. The tube and the Net clearly have not vanquished the book.

From 1965 to 1990, the number of symphony orchestras in the United States grew from 58 to nearly 300, opera companies from 27 to more than 150, nonprofit regional theaters from 22 to 500. Theater ticket sales are up. More American students are studying abroad.

A Rich and Diverse Culture

Of course, our culture is far more diverse, a fact that enriches or diminishes it, depending on your view. Some of the greatest cultural debates rage over the quick embrace of fleeting trends and the lack of respect for the great voices of the past. But we seem in fact to be blessed with a culture that can appreciate Mozart even as it enables women songwriters and singers to soar.

Laments about cultural decline echo through history. Listen to this 1808 European observer on the tragedy of the proliferation of popular novels through circulating libraries: "There is scarcely a street of the metropolis, or a village in the country, in which a circulating library may not be found: nor is there a corner of the empire, where the English language is understood, that has not suffered from the effects of this institution."

Today, we focus on some foul-mouthed rapper as if he were the sum total of all that we do and think, look at and listen to—as if he were somehow more representative of our culture than Duke Ellington or Martha Graham or Alfred Hitchcock.

Only history will sift out the great voices of our era, as it has from other eras. But we do have them, just as previous centuries had their Jerry Springer equivalents.

All of this is not to say we couldn't use some uplift. For exactly this purpose, poet and author Czeslaw Milosz assembled *A Book of Luminous Things*. It is an anthology of poetry—an art form that, as Milosz says, "cannot look at things of this earth other than as colorful, variegated and exciting, and so it cannot reduce life, with all its pain, horror, suffering and ecstasy, to a unified tonality of boredom or complaint."

A frequent review of the good things going on culturally and socially and a daily dip into Milosz's delightful collection: There's a fine cure for cultural pessimism, whatever direction it's coming from.

*"What the sensitivity folly is accomplishing
is the sort of leverage over people
commonly seen in a reign of terror."*

Political Correctness Threatens American Liberty

John Attarian

Liberal policies that advocate sensitivity about race and gender issues are often described as "politically correct" or "PC." Many people believe that society's emphasis on cultural sensitivity is oppressive because it punishes individuals for expressing opinions considered to be offensive to women and minorities. In the following viewpoint, freelance writer John Attarian argues that "leftist hypersensitivity" is now so pervasive that it poses a serious threat to individual liberty. He cites several examples in which people were unjustly punished or harassed for being culturally insensitive. What is most disturbing, Attarian concludes, is that the majority of Americans simply comply with these liberal demands to be politically correct.

As you read, consider the following questions:

1. According to Attarian, what happened when a Virginia woman called 911 to report that some black men were trying to break into her house?
2. What incident led to Mark Steenbergh being charged with assault and ethnic intimidation, according to the author?
3. In Attarian's opinion, why do most Americans submit to demands for so-called cultural sensitivity?

John Attarian, "Letter from Michigan: Be Sensitive—Or Else!" *Chronicles*, vol. 22, February 1998, pp. 36–37. Copyright © 1998 by The Rockford Institute. Reproduced by permission.

Horror stories about punishments for insensitive behavior on college campuses are old news. But leftist hypersensitivity has permeated everyday life in the real world as well. In Manassas, Virginia, a white woman called 911 at 3:08 A.M. to report that some black men—whom she referred to as "niggers"—were trying to break into her house. According to the *Detroit News*, the 911 dispatcher, also a white woman, sent police but went on to lecture the besieged woman: "The next time I would appreciate it if you would not call black gentlemen 'niggers,' OK? That offends me, and I don't like to hear it." She asked the distraught caller how she would like to be called "white trash."

As this case illustrates, the sensitivity police are everywhere. They are especially prevalent here in Michigan, where the sensitive are using intimidation and tyranny to flog the insensitive into line. For example, in May 1996, 57-year-old city councilwoman Gloria Sankuer of Warren (Michigan's third largest city) complained that the City Council's letterhead, referring to her as "councilman," was offensive. "This mistake makes Warren look sexist and backward," she said. "It needs to be fixed. It's a matter of what's proper." Warren had a four-year supply of this offending stationery. The council unanimously decided to expend it by sending all Warren city volunteers and unpaid board and committee members letters of thanks, costing over $400. All to placate one touchy feminist in a snit.

As Sankuer's case illustrates, the sensitivity mania opens up vast opportunities for busybodies. Ann Arborite Mark Hiselman, hearing of Sankuer's complaints, "drove 60 miles to be at the council meeting so he could offer an alternative voice." He tried unavailingly to get the council to adopt the gender-free "councilor" over "councilman," "councilwoman," and "council member."

At one time, this officious stranger, who does not even live in Warren, would have been deemed a public menace—which he is. By today's standards, Hiselman is in the *avant-garde* of righteousness. But if anybody's business is everybody's business, nobody is safe from molestation.

And then there is the Steenbergh case. On the night of September 11, 1996, Warren's mayor Mark Steenbergh confronted John Harris, a 16-year-old black male, near Harris's home. Earlier that day, Harris allegedly punched a 15-year-old girl, Wendy Smith, a friend of Steenbergh's daughter, in the face. Mayor Steenbergh decided to stick up for her and sought Harris out. He allegedly choked Harris, shoved him, and shouted "I'll get all you niggers" as he left the scene.

Within a week FBI agents were interviewing Harris's family. In November, Steenbergh's lawyer said, Michigan state police made a surprise after-hours raid, without a search warrant, on Warren City Hall looking for new evidence against Steenbergh. They found nothing. Apparently the sensitivity police wanted to get Mark Steenbergh badly enough to drag in the FBI and trample his constitutional rights with unreasonable searches and seizures.

Mayor Steenbergh was eventually charged with assault and ethnic intimidation. The maximum punishment for assault—a misdemeanor in Michigan—is a jail sentence of 90 days and a fine of $500. Ethnic intimidation, on the other hand, is a felony; those found guilty can be jailed for up to four years. Under Michigan's 1990 ethnic intimidation law, using a racial slur during a fight is not ethnic intimidation—but a fight or threat motivated by racial animosity is. The whole thing turns, then, on the motives of the miscreant—in other words, whether or not he is a racist.

After deliberating for one and a half hours, an all-white jury acquitted Steenbergh of all charges. Said jury foreman John Boyd, "It was the general feeling that some of the stories of the witnesses who supposedly were right there didn't make sense. Basically, it was the lack of credible evidence to support the charges."

Apparently, however, a lack of credible evidence is not enough to deter the FBI. Even though Steenbergh has been acquitted of state charges, as we go to press the FBI has not closed its case against him, leaving open the possibility that he may be prosecuted for violating Harris's civil rights, a federal offense.

The Andrea Ferrara Case

A more grotesque case is that of Wayne County Circuit Judge Andrea Ferrara. In February 1997, Ferrara's ex-husband,

Howard Tarjeft, released to the media tapes of telephone conversations in which a woman, supposedly Judge Ferrara, used slurs such as "nigger" and "Jew whore." The Detroit National Association for the Advancement of Colored People wrote to Wayne County Circuit Judge James Rashid, asking him to order Ferrara to resign from the bench. The Michigan Judicial Tenure Commission began investigating Ferrara. Meanwhile, her friends and supporters, including African-Americans and Jews, rallied to her defense. Ferrara claimed that she never made the remarks, that the tapes are fakes, and that Tarjeft is out to embarrass her.

Kelley. © 1999 by Steve Kelley. Reprinted with permission.

Tarjeft and Ferrara divorced bitterly in 1985. Tarjeft claims he made the tapes to "protect himself" during their vicious custody battle with Ferrara over their 14-year-old twin sons. He says he released them because he felt guilty about helping a racist get elected to the bench. Sure he did. Tarjeft released the tapes just days before he and Ferrara were scheduled to appear for a hearing over $12,000 that Ferrara claimed he owed her for back child support for their sons.

Asked by Judge Rashid to step down temporarily while the allegations of racism are being investigated, Ferrara announced in March that she was taking a three-month medical leave, until June 2. The Michigan Supreme Court suspended her with pay on May 6. On June 11, it appointed Vesta Svenson, former 36th District Court judge, to oversee a disciplinary hearing.

Based on the alleged racist remarks, Ferrara was charged with judicial misconduct. Hearings began in September. One of her 14-year-old sons testified that Ferrara had said "nigger" on several occasions. He also claimed that she had asked him if there was a way to destroy the infamous tapes. Ferrara denied her son's accusations, claiming Tarjeft had coached him to make her look bad, an allegation that Tarjeft denies. Understandably, Ferrara became emotional and accused the judge of "ruining my family" and "allowing my children to be used as pawns in an extortion scheme."

In a damaging blow to Ferrara, Avela Smith, an unemployed black woman, admitted that a letter praising Ferrara that she had sent to the *Michigan Chronicle* (a black newspaper) had been written by Ferrara for Smith's signature. Allan Sobel, the general counsel for Michigan's Judicial Tenure Commission, added a new misconduct charge: fabricating evidence. Other minorities, however, testified that they do not believe that Ferrara is a racist. As we go to press, Judge Svenson is preparing her report to the Judicial Tenure Commission, which will decide whether Ferrara should be reprimanded or removed from her job.

So we have a public servant under investigation, who has left a job she may very well lose, over alleged racial slurs in a private conversation with her ex-husband who has strong reasons for wanting to ruin her. True, nobody wants a biased judge—but a few words spoken in anger or frustration do not a racist make. One would think that a charge of judicial misconduct regarding race would concern whether or not Ferrara was unfair to blacks and other minorities in court—not words supposedly spoken among family. The whole thing smells fishy.

A naïf (that is, your average American) might say that the sensitivity crusade is much ado about nothing, and that this too shall pass when Americans' native good sense reasserts itself. But as Ayn Rand's villain Ellsworth Toohey observed, "there's always a purpose in nonsense. Don't bother to examine a folly—ask yourself only what it accomplishes." What the sensitivity folly is accomplishing is the sort of leverage over people commonly seen in a reign of terror.

Notice how much damage can be inflicted over accusations of racism and insensitivity, how quickly mere hearsay is seized on as proof positive, how quickly demonstrators and other such busybodies swing into action, how little recourse the accused have other than frightened denials and groveling for mercy. But perhaps the most disturbing thing is how little resistance there is to this reign of nonsense. If enough prospective victims defied it, the whole grotesque "sensitivity" jig would be up. But, confronted with demands that they slap their own faces with written apologies, Americans usually respond with slavish compliance. Typically, the accused parties strive to appease their persecutors; to either deny saying the offending things or to assure the public that they did not mean anything racist, sexist, or homophobic; to apologize, abjectly, extravagantly, endlessly; to confess that yes, they may have been insensitive; to scramble to make amends.

Rand said that "no injustice or exploitation can succeed for long without the sanction of the victim." It looks like these crusaders have Americans pegged: we really *are* insensitive—to threats to our liberty and affronts to our self-respect.

A Formula for Servility

In *The Gulag Archipelago*, Aleksandr Solzhenitsyn wrote perceptively of how the Moscow show trial defendants were weaklings, wanting above all to live pleasantly, and who therefore were cowed before Stalin's first blow was struck. A modern American's highest priority is an affluent, entertainment-rich lifestyle and social acceptance. To preserve his pleasant existence, he will trade away virtually everything else. Like the hapless Russians, "insensitive" white Americans uncannily resemble rabbits trembling with terror, not questioning the hawk's right to prey on them but merely hoping that the predator will pass them by this time. It is a formula for servility.

"In the face of political disagreement, isn't it best to start public conversations about the meaning of ideas like democracy, citizenship, and freedom, rather than yelling nazi at people with whom you disagree?"

The Issue of Political Correctness Deserves Open Discussion

Michael Bronski

Debates concerning political correctness should be discussed honestly and civilly, argues writer and activist Michael Bronski in the following viewpoint. Inspired by the social movements of the 1960s, political correctness faced a backlash in the 1990s as cultural critics and conservatives claimed that they felt oppressed by societal expectations to be sensitive to the needs of various minorities. This backlash, however, often trivialized the fact that women, gays, and minorities still faced discrimination. At the same time, those reacting against political correctness also addressed complex issues in which demands for cultural sensitivity clashed with the right to free speech. It is time for people to discuss such issues in a way that neither censors thought nor ignores real problems, the author concludes.

As you read, consider the following questions:

1. What well-known critics and media personalities joined the anti-PC backlash, according to the author?
2. In what specific instances are freedom of expression and cultural sensitivity at odds, according to Bronski?

Michael Bronski, "Sense and Sensitivity," *Z Magazine*, July/August 2002, pp. 16–18. Copyright © 2002 by *Z Magazine*. Reproduced by permission.

In the spring of 2002, in its nationwide chain of 311 stores, Abercrombie & Fitch began selling T-shirts featuring slant-eyed, coolie-hatted caricatures of Asian-American men. The humor teetered between burlesque and bathroom. The T-shirts carried aphorisms, such as "Wong Brothers Laundry Service"; "Two Wongs Can Make It White"; and "Wok-N-Bowl, Let The Good Times Roll."

These kinds of images of Asian-Americans thrived in the late 1800s and persisted in various forms, from Charlie Chan movies to TV series featuring "oriental" houseboys, until the 1960s. For at least 40 years, such stereotyping has been widely viewed as racist and offensive.

It's difficult to see how Abercrombie & Fitch—a clothier known for having its finger on the pulse of the wide, but shallow, pool of culturally hip consumers—could have thought these T-shirts, which retailed for $24.95, would sell. In remarks quoted widely in press reports, company spokesperson Hampton Carney, through Paul Wilmot Communications, A&F's public-relations firm, said, "We personally thought Asians would love this T-shirt."

But shortly after the shirts appeared on store shelves, Asian-American students at Stanford University protested the company's decision to sell the offending garments. The protests were quickly replicated on campuses nationwide. By April 18, 2002, just days after the shirts' appearance in some A&F stores, the company pulled the shirts from shelves as well as from its website. "We are very, very, very sorry," company spokesperson Carney told the media. "It's never been our intention to offend anyone. These graphic T-shirts were designed with the sole purpose of adding humor and levity to our fashion line."

As far as culture war battles go, this was a minor skirmish. But as a cultural moment it may herald a new level of discussion about popular culture politics. For many, the question of whether the Abercrombie & Fitch T-shirts are racist or insensitive is a no-brainer.

Yet in the early 1990s, a cultural critic like Camille Paglia might have rushed to the web pages of Salon and launched a defense of the shirts, claiming that they were the most recent artifacts in a long, rich tradition of racist caricatures that include Egyptian wall paintings, Picasso's use of African motifs, and "Mammy" cookie jars.

The Backlash Against Political Correctness

Paglia was not alone in her fury against political correctness (PC). During those same years, Katie Roiphe, author of *The Morning After: Sex, Fear, and Feminism* made a career of claiming that feminists made too big a deal of sexual assault and rape. Dinesh D'Souza, a founder of the conservative *Dartmouth Review* and author of *Illiberal Education: The Politics of Race and Sex on Campus*, complained that traditional Western culture and ideas were being driven from universities. Various shock-radio talk shows—Howard Stern's being the most famous—used racial, sexual, and ethnic stereotypes to both rile and amuse their listeners. The anti-PC backlash embodied a political and cultural response to many years of expecting people to be sensitive to the rights and feelings of a host of minorities. This sensitivity, nurtured in the liberation movements of the 1960s and early 1970s, had, by the Reagan years, run into a wall of "empathy fatigue" and overt antagonism.

If nothing else, the PC backlash sought to render social inequalities negligible. This charming period in American social relations saw anti-feminists declaiming, "Well, if they all want equality, why should I give up my seat to a pregnant woman on the bus?" and Republicans publicly ignoring statistics attributing an explosion of single motherhood among young African-American women to intractable poverty, so as not to ruffle their they-just-want-to-have-kids-to-become-welfare-cheats analysis. Complicated, honest, and empathetic discussion of these issues was squelched.

Indeed, the language used by those complaining of "political correctness run amok," to use a well-worn phrase from the culture wars, tried to turn the tables: they felt "oppressed" by political correctness. Rush Limbaugh complained endlessly about his archenemies, "the feminazis," and Paglia offhandedly referred to "leftist nazis." Howard Stern had a wide array of insults for people who found his humor offensive (typical remark: "I bet she hasn't gotten laid much lately").

It is no accident that so much of the anti-PC backlash centered on higher education and American intellectual life. Michelle Malkin, in her screed against the Abercrombie & Fitch protesters, claimed that they had learned their tactics from "their professors" ("It's Ethnic Extortionism 101"). Paglia, a tenured professor at the University of the Arts in Philadelphia, blamed PC on postmodern theories and French intellectuals. Limbaugh, a millionaire, claimed to speak for the common man against "know-it-all intellectuals."

Common Decency

Well, I admit it. I spend a fair amount of time and effort trying my best to be politically correct. I have never, for example, during a polite conversation, asked a heterosexual to explain to me about her activities in the bedroom, although they might seem exotic to me. And it's been years since I've told a joke that begins, "a priest, a rabbi, and a minister. . . ."

I have come under a fair amount of criticism for this behavior, and become the butt of many jokes in society these days. But I can't for the life of me figure out why, since I believe that what some deride as "political correctness" is really only a caricatured description of what I always defined as common decency; a variation on the Levitical precept that what is hateful to you, you should not do to others.

Rebecca T. Alpert, *Tikkun*, March/April 1996.

Even privileged Ivy Leaguers like Roiphe (Harvard) and D'Souza (Dartmouth) railed against new intellectual constructs and forms of thinking that had supplemented more traditional ones. The heart of the anti-PC backlash was profoundly anti-intellectual. The charge "Don't be so PC" generally means, as Howard Stern so beautifully puts it, "Oh, shut up."

It was a stroke of genius for the right to appropriate the term "political correctness" (which had been used in a self-deprecating way by progressives for years) to dismiss minorities' concerns as a form of fascistic social-thought control. It was a one-size-fits-all put-down that could be applied as easily to Spike Lee's movies as to a speech by a moderate feminist like Gloria Steinem or to basic constitutional arguments for anti-gay-discrimination bills.

Yet many fights over "political correctness" have focused

on important and complicated issues, such as speech codes on college campuses; freedom-of-association issues, such as whom the Boy Scouts or the organizers of St. Patrick's Day parades get to exclude; and constitutional questions concerning how far free speech can go before it becomes hate speech or incites violence.

Even all-American projects like boycotts have come under scrutiny, as when both right- and left-wingers debated the appropriateness of conservative Christians' economic boycott of the TV show *Ellen* or liberals' boycott of the *Dr. Laura* show. In the face of political disagreement, isn't it best to start public conversations about the meaning of ideas like democracy, citizenship, and freedom, rather than yelling nazi at people with whom you disagree?

It would be a grievous mistake to downplay the importance of these cultural debates. The anti-PC backlash was a deeply felt response to changes taking place so quickly that they were bound to encounter resistance. In the constitutional democracy under which we live, there is an ongoing struggle to balance First Amendment rights to free speech with efforts to sustain civil society. Freedom of expression and cultural sensitivity are often at odds, whether the issue involves the freedom to burn a cross in a black neighborhood; the rights of Nazis to march in predominantly Jewish Skokie, Illinois; the rights of anti-abortion groups to picket abortion clinics and place death-target lists of physicians who perform abortions on their web pages; or the rights of people to use racial or homophobic slurs on the airwaves. Or, for that matter, on T-shirts.

The Need for Honest Discussion

As a culture, we've rarely discussed such issues openly, honestly, and civilly. To be sure, there are exceptions to that rule, such as Randall Kennedy's book *Nigger*, an extraordinary explication of the social and political uses of that most contentious of words and Spike Lee's film *Bamboozled*, a shocking and painfully entertaining history of racist images in popular culture.

But what has been clear throughout the last 15 years is that the lines between freedom and respect, and honest expression and hurtful utterance, become blurred when people vindicate speech that others find painful by claiming it's just a joke. That assertion trivializes the issue and willfully ignores the fact that all jokes mask serious meaning.

Abercrombie & Fitch's willingness to admit a mistake—that it overstepped an important boundary and that it should have taken people's feelings into consideration—could signal a shift in a culture marked by diminished empathy and heightened defensiveness. Maybe this is a step in the right direction, away from political correctness and its dissenters and toward really looking at how people try to live their lives with both humor and dignity.

Periodical Bibliography

The following articles have been selected to supplement the diverse views presented in this chapter.

Richard Alleva	"The Rap on 'Rap': Yo, Where's the Melody?" *Commonweal*, June 15, 2001.
William J. Bennett	"What Hath the Beatles Wrought? Rock-&-Roll and the Collapse of Authority," *American Enterprise*, May/June 1997.
Christian Century	"Moral Collapse?" March 10, 1999.
Tyler Cowen	"Is Our Culture in Decline?" *CATO Policy Report*, September/October 1998.
William Norman Grigg	"In Sade's Shadow," *New American*, April 9, 2001.
Kimberly A. Hendrickson	"The Survival of Moral Federalism," *Public Interest*, Summer 2002.
Wendy Kaminer	"Law and Marriage," *American Prospect*, July 2, 2001.
Everett Carll Ladd	"The American Way—Civic Engagement—Thrives," *Christian Science Monitor*, March 1, 1999.
John Lukacs	"To Hell with Culture," *Chronicles*, July 2001.
Jennifer Roback Morse	"The Moral Roots of Liberty and Prosperity," *American Enterprise*, July 2001.
Christina Hoff Sommers	"Why Johnny Can't Tell Right from Wrong," *American Outlook*, Summer 1998.
David C. Stolinsky	"Our Titanic Nonjudgmentalism," *New Oxford Review*, April 2000.
Tomislav Sunic	"Sixty-Eighters," *Chronicles*, March 1999.
James B. Twitchell	"It's a Material World, and That's OK," *Wilson Quarterly*, Spring 1999.
Anne Wortham	"America's Cultural-Institutional Core," *World & I*, November 2001.

CHAPTER 3

What Political and Cultural Influences Benefit Society?

Chapter Preface

In discussions about politics, moral values, and culture, the issue of religion inevitably emerges. Social conservatives, for example, often claim that a moral society is by definition a religious society, and that the growth of secularism is detrimental to America's political and cultural life. Basic ethical principles stem from a belief in a supreme being who has the power and authority to enforce moral standards, contends Christian apologetics professor John M. Frame. "We cannot be obligated to atoms, or gravity, or evolution, or time, or chance; we can be obligated only to persons. . . . An *absolute* standard, one without exceptions, one that binds everybody, must be based on loyalty to a person great enough to deserve such respect. Only God meets that description." Frame insists that any moral system constructed by nonbelievers is dangerously unstable because it has no higher authority as its foundation. "If we are to reverse our cultural decline," he concludes, "we should begin to take God much more seriously, in parenting, education, and public dialogue."

Secularists, on the other hand, maintain that humans can agree on ethical standards without presuming that morality is ordained and enforced by a supreme being. They generally believe that moral laws were created by humans so that society could function peacefully and efficiently. Furthermore, as Paul Kurtz, chair of the Council for Secular Humanism, points out, religious belief does not ensure morality: "So many infamous deeds have been perpetrated in the name of God—the Crusades, the Inquisition, religious-inspired terrorism . . . that it is difficult to blithely maintain that belief in God guarantees morality. It is thus the height of intolerance to insist that only those who accept religious dogma are moral." Empathy for others is the ethical principle that holds true for both atheists and believers—and thus, humanists contend, empathy should be upheld as society's guiding moral standard.

Disagreement about which beliefs and cultural influences strengthen American society persists. The following chapter presents differing opinions on the effects of political ideology, religion, and multiculturalism in the United States.

"Progressives have a long tradition of fighting for values like equality, civil liberties, opportunity, and justice."

Political Progressivism Should Be Promoted

Paul Wellstone and Bill Dauster

Political progressives focus on enhancing popular participation in politics and on using governmental means to improve the human condition, contend Paul Wellstone and Bill Dauster in the following viewpoint. Labor laws, social security, electoral reforms, health insurance, and civil rights victories are just some of the national achievements that resulted from progressive efforts, the authors point out. Currently, progressives need to push for increased access to child care, health care, living wages, and quality education. They must also fight cynicism as they continue to champion grassroots political participation and social justice, the authors conclude. Before his death in 2002, Wellstone was a Democratic senator from Minnesota. Dauster was a counselor to Wellstone.

As you read, consider the following questions:
1. In the authors' opinion, why were Democrats successful in the November 1998 elections?
2. According to Franklin Roosevelt, quoted by the authors, what is the real test of political progress?
3. According to Wellstone and Dauster, what must a political party do if it wishes to thrive?

Paul Wellstone and Bill Dauster, "We Cannot Buy Golden Opportunities with Tin-Cup Budgets," *The Progressive*, vol. 63, January 1999, p. 44. Copyright © 1999 by The Progressive, Inc. Reproduced by permission.

From the beginning of the twentieth century, the progressive movement sought a better society and better government. The movement . . . advocated laws to shield workers and consumers from unchecked industrialization and corporate monopolies. They fought for open and honest government and to broaden popular participation. And they advanced the ethic of improving the human condition.

We have so come to rely on what they accomplished that we take their achievements for granted. Progressives led the fight for child labor laws, the eight-hour day, tax reform, old age security, unemployment compensation, a minimum wage, occupational health and safety, and health insurance. Progressives gave us the universal right to vote, the direct election of Senators, the initiative, the referendum, and the recall.

The progressive movement also manifested a confident belief in the affirmative development of society. Many progressives strove to build "The Beloved Community," a corner of God's kingdom right here on Earth. We need to rededicate ourselves not just to progressive policies and programs but to progressive values, to a conception of public life that is democratic and fulfilling.

People are still looking for progressive change. It's time to reclaim our confidence. The midterm elections in 1998 were a lesson for Republicans. Voters told Congressional Republicans that they did not want to hire 535 private eyes and prosecutors. Congressional Republicans failed to show how they would advance the interests of working families. Most Democrats showed that they cared about bread-and-butter issues—education, health care, and Social Security. Because they fought for progressive goals, Democrats benefited as in no other midterm election in memory.

But the 1998 elections were a lesson for Democrats, too. Unfortunately, a lot of Washington, D.C., Democrats think the lesson was: Our message was better, so we won, end of story. But it's not about "message"—a word that describes the shallow incrementalism of the Bill Clinton era.

In the long run, Democrats cannot inspire voters' imagination and regain power merely by appealing to whichever group of swing voters this year's consultants make fashionable.

In the long run, the success of a political movement depends on doing something of consequence. Progressives must step to the plate with real proposals again.

The Lesson of 1998

For years now, Democrats have been downsizing our policy agenda. Instead of universal health coverage, Democrats have focused on patients' protections. Instead of recruiting the vast new corps of teachers our schools desperately need, Democrats have settled for a modest 30,000 new teachers. Democrats risk becoming conspirators in support of the status quo.

Democrats should find no reassurance in winning half of the votes cast by the 37 percent of voters who turned out in November 1998. It was great to see such progressives as Wisconsin's Russ Feingold and California's Barbara Boxer win elections. But don't lose sight of the 63 percent hole in the electorate nationwide. When almost two-thirds of eligible voters choose not to vote, something is seriously wrong. The nonvoters are telling us they are disillusioned with their choices. They are saying that no one speaks for them.

The election's lesson was not just that the Republican Party should wake up, but that Democrats should, too. Vast majorities of the electorate found no reason to vote for the status quo. Both parties ignore that lesson at their own risk. If they continue to ignore it, third-party victories like Jesse Ventura's populist surprise in Minnesota will become more frequent.

As the Irishman Charles Stewart Parnell said more than a century ago, "No man has a right to say to his country—thus far shall thou go and no farther." Democrats need to return to their progressive roots, to an agenda promising real change with real positive consequences for working families.

Incremental policies will not bridge the broad and growing chasm that divides a prospering, affluent group from the vast majority of Americans who continue to struggle to make ends meet.

We need to advance a coordinated strategy to improve wages for working Americans, not just the few at the top. To do so, we need to raise the minimum wage and enact living-wage policies, such as those in Minneapolis and other American cities today.

We need to enact labor-law reform so that working people can regain their bargaining power.

And we need to do more to develop workers' skills throughout their lifetimes.

As Franklin Roosevelt said, "The test of our progress is not whether we add more to the abundance of those who have much; it is whether we provide enough for those who have too little."

Addressing the Needs of Ordinary Citizens

Yes, Democrats should support changes like reducing class size and repairing schools. But in education, as in other areas, we need to do more. Just when more than a million teachers are nearing retirement, the coming decade will see an 11 percent increase in the number of high school students. This provides a golden opportunity to inspire, train, and hire into the public schools of our communities a new generation of bright, young teachers fresh with new ideas and new energy. But this nation cannot buy golden opportunities with tin-cup budgets like those we have now. We need to inspire a campaign to bring smart and creative young Americans into teaching. We need to champion the vision of a new education century.

We also need to address families' biggest and most expensive concerns—child care and health care. Without quality child care, many parents are now forced to work in shifts; they and their children are robbed of time together as a family. We need to take bold steps to expand the availability of child care for the 8.5 million children now eligible to receive assistance who do not get that aid.

Above and beyond the lack of patient protections, health care remains a crisis for many Americans. In1990, fewer than 14 percent of Americans went without health insurance. Today, more than 16 percent are uninsured. Even assuming good economic times, close to 48 million Americans will have no health insurance coverage by the year 2005. Around the country, many elderly Americans pay more than 30 percent of their monthly budget on prescription drug costs alone.

Progressives must call for insuring the uninsured, guaranteeing affordable, comprehensive insurance for all, requiring quality health care, and covering prescription drug costs under Medicare. Washington took the issue of universal coverage off the table. Progressives need to put it back.

The Progressive Tradition

Both parties have succumbed to the cultural temptation—the Republicans to the evangelical right, the Democrats to the politically correct left. Perhaps, especially with economic troubles apparently ahead, the time has arrived for American liberalism to return to fundamentals. With [the George W. Bush] administration so firmly in the hands of the corporate community, has the time not come for the revival of the Progressive tradition?

How to define the Progressive tradition? Let me cite a text. Progressivism sprang from the cities while Populism was an agrarian movement; but the Populists prepared the way for the Progressives by breaking with the basic Jeffersonian dogma that the government that governs least governs best. Fearful of the rising power of the large corporations, the Populists declared in their 1892 platform: "We believe that the powers of government—in other words, of the people—should be expanded . . . to the end that oppression, injustice, and poverty shall eventually cease in the land."

Arthur M. Schlesinger Jr., *American Prospect*, April 23, 2001.

Finally, money prowls the corridors of the Capitol and the halls of the White House. If we do not take big money out of politics, then that money will divert, frustrate, and ultimately deny our nation's historic movement toward economic justice.

Clean Money Campaign Reform, which has already passed in Massachusetts, Arizona, Maine, and Vermont, provides real hope for driving big money out of election campaigns and inviting ordinary citizens back into effective participation in politics.

Renewing Democracy

But we must reform not just politics. We must renew democracy itself. We have to fight cynicism and inertia and restore faith in the advancement of our country.

To do that, progressives need to rejoin the debate over an overarching set of values in government. For too long, we have left that battlefield to the right. Progressives have a long tradition of fighting for values like equality, civil liberties, opportunity, and justice. We need to recall the values that have spurred broad-based efforts like the civil-rights movement—values that today can spark a new movement for social justice.

We must sound the clarion call to improve the human condition. As British Prime Minister Harold Wilson once said, "The only human institution which rejects progress is the cemetery." If a political party wants to avoid being buried, it must become a champion of change.

Let us make the Democratic Party the party of the people again.

Education, living-wage jobs, child care, health care, electoral reform, and public values: The Republicans don't get it. Do the Democrats? Our job as progressives is to make sure that they do.

Let us move ahead boldly into a new Progressive Century.

"Conservatives resolve arguments in favor of the individual rather than the collective, of clear standards of judgment rather than relativistic measures, of personal responsibility rather than the interplay of vast social forces."

Political Conservatism Should Be Promoted

Policy Review

In the following viewpoint, the editors of *Policy Review* define ideological conservatism and propose strategies for enhancing its influence in the twenty-first century. Conservatives champion individual liberty, personal responsibility, free enterprise, international self-reliance, and minimal government intervention in Americans' lives. The authors contend that conservatism aims to defeat radicalism and offer solid alternatives to liberalism—an ideology that has dominated American politics for decades but has ultimately proven ineffectual. Serious, deliberate thinking and self-scrutiny will benefit conservative thinkers in the years to come. *Policy Review* is a bimonthly journal of conservative opinion.

As you read, consider the following questions:

1. According to the editors of *Policy Review*, how do conservatives propose to make the future better?
2. Who are the typical figures in conservative intellectual culture today, according to the authors?

For better or worse, modern ideological conservatism constitutes a completed body of thought. We need not try to settle the issue of how it came to completion, an exercise in intellectual history a bit beyond the scope of these reflections, to note the fact. There was a time, coming to a close perhaps a decade ago, when those of us who took an interest in the development of conservative ideology eagerly reached for our newly arrived periodicals and newly published books in the expectation of finding bold new insights into vexing problems, some of which we did not even realize were problems. This was an exciting time—conservative ideology was a work in progress, and the task had urgency, vitality, and freshness. Part of the task was the development of a thorough critique of liberal and radical ideology and the effects these had throughout our politics and culture. But conservative ideology was not merely negative—merely based in criticism. It had a positive component as well, laying claim to a future it proposed to make better through the defeat of radicalism, the rejection of liberalism, and the implementation of conservative ideas in the policy arena.

Basic Conservatism

This period of intellectual ferment is over. In a way, that is a tribute to its success. One can say of ideological conservatism nowadays that, in general, it knows what the important questions are and it knows the answers to those questions. There remains much detail to work out, but the outlines are clear. Conservatives resolve arguments in favor of the individual rather than the collective, of clear standards of judgment rather than relativistic measures, of personal responsibility rather than the interplay of vast social forces, of the market rather than government economic intervention, of international strength and self-reliance rather than empty promises of security. The federal government is, in general, too big, taxing too much of the wealth of Americans, doing too many unnecessary and often counterproductive things that get in the way of economic growth, to say nothing of personal liberty. Even as it has indulged in frivolity, the federal government has been neglectful of the security of Americans in its rush to disarm after the successful conclusion of the Cold War. Meanwhile, a debased high and popular culture shows few signs of recovery.

Among conservatives, one is hard-pressed to find any disagreement on these basic issues. The real questions, instead, are whether, when, and how the American political process will make good on the promises of conservatism. In certain respects, this is a tribute to the triumph of conservative ideology. In the absence of its searching critique of liberalism and its advancement of an alternative vision, it seems unlikely that the old liberal dominance would have faded as it has. The practical import of this triumph is that conservative ideology is no longer merely a theoretical matter. Conservatives would like to implement it, to substitute their ideas for the dead hand of liberalism that guided our politics for decades. The principal activity of ideological conservatism . . . takes place not in the realm of ideas, but in the world of politics.

The Conservative Intellectual Culture

The characteristic figures of conservative intellectual culture are no longer professors and intellectuals. The characteristic figures are lawyers and journalists. This, as much as anything, is an indication of how far conservatism has come.

Making the law and reporting on how the law is or isn't getting made: In some ways, these seem the principal activities of idea-minded conservatives nowadays. Once again, this may be a product of the success of the intellectual endeavor, over the years, in asking and answering the basic questions. But there are no more basic questions to ask and answer, or so it seems, and so it seems neither inappropriate nor terribly significant that for those interested in the life of the mind these days, at least outside the academy, action consists of either a seat at the table where the big decisions are being made; or a place at the peephole into the room with the table, in order to describe it for others (and second-guess it).

The conservative intellectual culture reflects the broader media culture around us. That broader culture now worships two principal deities: Much and Quick. Our culture produces an extraordinary volume of information for anyone interested in consuming information. Never have so many had so much access to so much, nor so quickly. What is a media culture to do in the age of the Internet and 24-hour cable programming on politics? The answer has been: Go along with it. In addition to a new breed of on-line "magazines" whose content changes from hour to hour, we have seen biweekly, weekly, and daily publications break out of their traditional "news cycle" to give us the benefit of their reporting and analysis as soon as they can post it on their web sites. Conservatism, for its part, is now propagated as much by simultaneous e-mail transmission as by any other medium. To be au courant [current] is to answer a liberal argument made on a morning cable show by early afternoon. It may, however, be an indication of how well-formed conservative thought is that it can propagate answers so quickly.

The Questions to the Answers

Is anything wrong with this? On one hand, no. In the first place, there is no undoing the profusion of cable or the availability of the Internet. We live in our time. It would be the height of folly to cede such powerful tools as the Internet and cable to people out to do in the conservative project. As long as these media are available, it only makes sense to seize them and use them the best one can. In the second place, the sometimes-rote quality of the propagation of conservatism and conservative positions is hardly the product of imposition of intellectual orthodoxy by some central committee taking as its charge the enforcement of discipline among the cadres. There is no such committee. Instead, the familiar quality of conservatism is a product of widespread agreement among thoughtful people. Its completed character is testimony to the sway of reason among reasonable people.

But is a swift and certain conservatism, even if such a conservatism is essential, actually sufficient? Here, there is reason to pause.

The long-term success of conservative ideology depends on how well that ideology understands and describes the world and predicts outcomes in it. If, in point of fact, conservative ideology is perfectly formed at present, then there is no particular risk in the current state of conservative in-

America's Founding Principles

Our greatest, indeed unconquerable, assets are embodied in the [conservative] principles of the American Founding. Here they are: the rule of law, individual rights, the guarantee of property, and our common American identity—the last also being the repository of our moral code. During the next election cycle, the nation should submit candidates, issues, positions, and statutes—both previously enacted and to be proposed—to the simple test of these principles. We ought to use them as a do-no-harm screen. Only the candidates, political positions, and legislative items that pass through that screen should receive further consideration.

For two centuries, our two major political parties have found more than enough upon which to disagree without abandoning these principles. John F. Kennedy was committed to them no less than Dwight D. Eisenhower, whom he replaced. Jimmy Carter was no less committed to them than Gerald R. Ford, whom he defeated.

They are America's principles, and America will not survive without them.

Balint Vazsonyi, *American Outlook*, Winter 1999.

tellectual culture. But if not, then what? And how will conservatives know?

The liberal experience should send a cautionary signal to conservatives. Liberalism as an ideology proved remarkably disinclined to engage in self-examination. The intellectual energy of liberalism was largely taken up in a decades-long argument between the go-fast liberals and the one-step-at-a-time liberals. Liberalism had no particular response to external pressure, either in the form of the failure of the world to act in accordance with its expectations or in the form of the conservative intellectual critique of liberalism during the heyday of the formation of conservative ideology. Liberalism, comfortable in the wielding of political power, simply did so—until there came the point at which it lost political power as a result of the bankruptcy, insufficiency, and stubborn wrong-headedness of its ideas.

Liberalism would surely have been better off had some substantial number of its most talented adherents been able or willing to take a step back from their ideological certainty and re-examine their premises in the light of real-world results. (One could say that some liberals did take this road, only to become conservatives; on the other hand, it is hardly obvious that the only alternative to liberalism is ideological conservatism.)

Conservatives should profit from this error. Some of them ought to take it as a project of some urgency to step back from the now hurly-burly world of conservative political and intellectual culture and take a long, hard, detailed look at conservatism. The alternative is merely the assumption that all is well. That is a dangerous assumption. Even if all is well, it is better to say so on the basis of serious self-scrutiny than on a whim, or worse, out of the ideological conviction that all must be well. And suppose all is not well. Suppose one or another problem becomes apparent. There is at least a possibility that such problems as arise can be addressed and corrected before their steady accretion threatens the totality of the project of conservative governance. If ideological conservatism now is relatively self-confident in the conviction that it has the right answers to the important questions, the time has come for the right questions about the answers.

Time to Think

One thing is certain. No serious conservative self-scrutiny will arise spontaneously from the current media culture. Rather, such scrutiny can only be a product of a deliberate decision on the part of some number of serious people to take the time to think about some pretty serious things. And the product of their deliberations will not be the least suited to delivery via sound bite or e-mail.

They will write essays. These essays will be published in a magazine that has made a deliberate decision to make its stand outside the news cycle. In a culture increasingly given to Much and Quick and more and faster, this magazine will take the radically contrarian view that seriousness necessitates deliberation, and that an article that can be read with profit and enjoyment a year or two or a dozen after it first appears is potentially at least as valuable a thing as all the e-mail traffic in between. This magazine, in turn, will be read by people who appreciate the limitations of the media culture of Much and Quick—and the perhaps-hidden dangers this culture poses to conservatism. This magazine and its audience will, in short, constitute the dynamic element of modern conservative thinking.

The creation of modern conservative ideology was an exercise in ideas—in many cases, ideas about the consequences of an older set of ideas, those of liberalism. But conservatism is no longer merely about ideas, because conservative ideas are having consequences of their own. The success or failure of conservatism, in the long run, will depend on how well conservatism understands those consequences and adapts to them. . . .

In a world of ephemera, it is time for some number of people to devote their energies and attention to matters of lasting consequence.

*"Religion is alive and well in America—
and a good deal of what it says and does is
strikingly progressive."*

Religious Progressivism
Benefits Society

Richard Parker

Discussions of religion and politics often focus on conservative opinion and the agenda of the Christian right. However, as Richard Parker explains in the following viewpoint, religious progressivism is a vital, albeit unrecognized, force in American life. Left-leaning religious believers in the Protestant, Catholic, and Jewish traditions are actively participating in struggles for wage reform, labor rights, improved low-income housing, health care, and ecological sustainability. Moreover, the denominational teachings of the major religions emphasize the importance of such progressive ideals as economic justice and human rights. Parker is a senior fellow and adjunct lecturer at Harvard University's Kennedy School. He is also the author of *The Myth of the Middle Class* and *Mixed Signals: The Future of Global Television News.*

As you read, consider the following questions:
1. According to Parker, what progressive victories have been won by Clergy and Laity United for Economic Justice (CLUE)?
2. What is Call to Renewal, according to the author?
3. In what ways have liberals misread the Christian right, in Parker's opinion?

Richard Parker, "Progressive Politics and, Uh . . . , God," *American Prospect*, vol. 11, January 17, 2000, pp. 32–37. Copyright © 2000 by *American Prospect*. Reproduced by permission.

When I tell politically progressive friends that I've started teaching a course at Harvard about religion's impact on American politics and public policy, I usually face one of two responses.

The first is an awkward silence—and a quick change of subject. The second is also awkward but comes with an anxiously knowing, usually sotto voce, "So you're doing abortion and the Christian right—that sort of thing, yes?" When I explain that, no, in fact I'm devoting only a week of the course to the religious right and that I barely mention abortion, it's usually back to awkward silence again—and the search for a new subject.

In the right mood, I'm sympathetic to my friends' reactions. After all, what comes to mind when someone mentions religion and politics nowadays? Aren't Jerry Falwell, Pat Robertson, Gary Bauer, anti-abortion picketers, and anti-gay marchers probably the first images? Or is it perhaps former president Bill Clinton, lachrymose at a Washington prayer breakfast in 1999, earnestly "repenting" his affair with Monica Lewinsky? More recently, what about the House Republicans voting that schools post the Ten Commandments in answer to gun violence? Or the discomforting sudden embrace of religion by the crop of presidential candidates and their minions in the year 2000?

It's not a list designed to warm progressive hearts. But as I've come to discover, it's far from all we need to know or care about American religion. Contrary to what many may think, religion is alive and well in America—and a good deal of what it says and does is strikingly progressive.

What Progressives Should Know

Of course, religion has been ever present in American life. Alexis de Tocqueville was hardly the first to point to its centrality to our civic life and politics, and even Karl Marx saw we were unique in this respect. "America," he wrote, "is preeminently the country of religiosity," with, he admitted, "a fresh and vigorous vitality."

No one who reflects even for a moment on abolition, suffrage, temperance, the Progressive era, or various utopian, labor, and reform movements—or, more recently, on civil rights, the Vietnam era, or the 1980s' battles over Central America and nuclear weapons—can miss the vital role of religious leaders, visions, and communities in each of these transformative struggles.

But what about today?

Here's what surprises a lot of my progressive friends:

In Los Angeles, California, you'll find the progressive religious tradition alive in Clergy and Laity United for Economic Justice (CLUE), a coalition of ministers, priests, and rabbis that proved decisive in getting the city's landmark living-wage ordinance passed in 1997.

Since then, CLUE has been working with local labor unions to organize low-wage workers in hotels, airports, and restaurants. In the spring of 1999, CLUE won local celebrity—and a key victory for workers at posh L.A. hotels—by organizing a march down Beverly Hills' Rodeo Drive in the midst of Easter week and Passover. As bystanders gaped from behind the store windows of Fendi, Armani, and the like, 150 rabbis, Catholic priests, and Protestant ministers in full flowing robes filed down the street. At the head of the procession, they carried a 25-foot-long banner declaring "ALL RELIGIONS BELIEVE IN JUSTICE." "Shoppers froze in their tracks," one participant remembers, and local TV and radio crews converged on the scene. The procession stopped first in front of two hotels that had agreed, after a long struggle, to sign the new union contract. Here they deposited bowls filled with milk and honey—biblical symbols of the promised land—along with baskets of Easter lilies. But to a hotel that refused to sign the new contract, they instead brought bitter herbs, the Passover symbol of slavery. Within three weeks, all the targeted hotels signed hefty new contracts with their workers.

You'll find that same sort of dynamism in the Greater Boston Interfaith Organization (GBIO). At its founding meeting in 1999, nearly 5,000 people heard inner-city black Pentecostal ministers, suburban Unitarian and Episcopalian clergy, a rabbi, an imam, and Boston's Archbishop Bernard Cardinal Law, all preaching a new era of multiracial, multiethnic, faith-led urban renewal. Nearly 100 congregations, union locals, and community groups have now begun working together to improve low-income housing, city schools, and job conditions for new immigrants.

In Washington, D.C., a progressive evangelical group called Sojourners regularly challenges conservative evangelicals on issues ranging from income, gender, and racial equality to support for organized labor and the environment. In 1996, the group—which had existed for a quarter of a century—launched an organizing project named Call to Renewal. Across the country, Call to Renewal has come into dozens of communities at the invitation of local church groups (and even politicians) to stop gang violence, foster urban renewal, help secure jobs for minority youth, and fight drug abuse. Evangelicals have a long tradition of concern for the poor, notes the Reverend Emory Searcy, national field organizer for the group. But to Searcy, a black Baptist minister, too many evangelicals "got hijacked by the right" in recent years. "We're just asking them to recapture their own history.". . .

Religion and Social Justice

Working out of offices at the Cathedral of St. John the Divine on New York's Upper West Side, the National Religious Partnership for the Environment (NRPE) has been pressing churches and synagogues to take up global warming, toxic pollution, rain forest destruction, and ecological sustainability as part of their everyday ministry. And not just by "having guys with collars at a press conference," insists Paul Gorman, the group's director. With $10 million from the Pew Charitable Trusts, Nathan Cummings, MacArthur, and other foundations, NRPE is trying to make each denomination's teachings about the environment integral to what is preached from its pulpits, what is taught in its Sunday schools and seminaries, and what guides its institutional behavior. . . .

Faith-based groups from Delaware to Georgia are helping to organize thousands of mainly black and Latino workers in the enormous, low-wage poultry-processing industry. This is an industry, according to the Department of Labor, in which 60 percent of plants regularly violate wage and hour laws and workers who try to join unions are routinely harassed or fired. Working together as the Poultry Justice Alliance, these groups use well-publicized local rallies and prayer vigils (as well as lobbying pressure brought by their national denominations) to help the industry's workers secure basic labor rights. The Poultry Justice Alliance, in turn, is just one of nearly four dozen local faith-based groups in 25 states that coordinate their efforts on behalf of workers in sweatshops, nursing homes, and the hotel industry through the Chicago-based National Interfaith Committee for Worker Justice.

America's Catholic bishops—mainly through their Catholic Campaign for Human Development—contribute between $10 million and $20 million a year to grass-roots progressive groups around the country, working on everything from inner-city community renewal in Chicago to tenant organizing in California. And millions more flow each year from Catholic orders like the Maryknolls and Jesuits as well as mainline Protestant denominations and liberal Jewish groups. One guidebook for progressive activists, for example, lists nearly eight dozen major religious funding sources that might support their work.

In short, there's a great deal going on in America's religious life that liberals should know more about—and support. Yet the fact is we often do neither.

God and Country

Garry Wills thinks that the ignorance of liberals and intellectuals generally about American religion reflects a deeper blindness. In *Under God*, he's blunt about his views:

> The learned have their superstitions, prominent among them a belief that superstition is evaporating. . . . Every time religiosity catches the attention of intellectuals, it is as if a shooting star has appeared in the sky. One could hardly guess, from this, that nothing has been more stable in our history, nothing less budgeable, than religious belief and practice.

The charge has a decided edge to it, but if you look at Gallup's nearly half a century of polling data about Americans and religion, it's not hard to see why Wills feels the way he does. According to Gallup:

- Nine out of 10 Americans say they've never doubted the existence of God.
- Eight out of 10 Americans believe they'll be called be-

fore God on Judgment Day to answer for their sins.

- Seven in 10 say they're current church or synagogue members.
- Four in 10 say they worship at least weekly (six in 10 say at least monthly) as members of a religious congregation.

All this cuts against the confident belief many once held that religion in the United States was in terminal decline, thanks to the secularizing forces of urbanization, industrialization, scientific explanation, and consumer culture. . . .

Liberalism's Core Values

That liberals and the Pope have more in common on socio-economic issues than you might think isn't just coincidence. Many of liberalism's core values—whether help for the downtrodden or support for peace—derive from the Judeo-Christian tradition. Liberals who disdain religion are inadvertently acting like embarrassed adolescents who shun their own parents. For whether or not you believe Jesus was resurrected, he still offers a model for a life of radical social justice. Whether you believe God or men wrote the Bible, it too speaks to how we live.

Amy Waldman, *Washington Monthly*, December 1995.

But if Americans remain overwhelmingly religious, our faiths still come in a rainbow of colors. Roughly a quarter of Americans tell pollsters they're mainline Protestants, another quarter that they're fundamentalist Protestants, and a quarter that they're Catholics. About 10 percent are black Protestants, 2 percent are Jews, 2 percent are Mormons, 1 percent are Orthodox Christians, and another 1 or 2 percent identify with "other religions"—mostly Islam, Buddhism, and Hinduism. (Barely one-tenth of Americans say they have no religious identity.)

At first glance, of course, those numbers make America an overwhelmingly Christian country—more Christian, in fact, than India is Hindu, Israel is Jewish, or Latin America is Catholic. However, that massive "Christian majority," as the Christian right likes to call it, is—and always has been—deeply and fractiously divided. What's more, the divisions aren't just liturgical or theological. There are also sharp—

and long-enduring—differences in the political and social beliefs of the denominations.

Political analyst Kevin Phillips's latest book *The Cousins' Wars* traces the origin of the divides among progressive, liberal, and conservative Protestant denominations all the way back to the English Revolution, then follows its recurring patterns through the American Revolution and Civil War.

In America's post–Civil War period, science and industrialization led to new divisions as well as the deepening of older ones, as the defeated South—still home today to the majority of America's fundamentalists—hardened into religious as well as political conservatism.

Meanwhile, mainline Protestants openly embraced not only religious ecumenism but the idea that science was reconcilable with religious belief. That openness in turn fueled support for the Social Gospel movement, which was central in popularizing the reformist idea of government during the Progressive era.

Likewise, modern Catholic interest in liberal politics and public policy can trace its own genesis to the nineteenth-century encyclical Rerum Novarum, to Father John Ryan's turn-of-the-twentieth-century work on living wages, and to Vatican II in the 1960s. In the midst of the Reagan era, the Catholic Church's powerful voice on social-justice issues was epitomized by the U.S. bishops' influential and prophetic declarations on economic justice and nuclear war.

Faith and Progressivism

Over the past 20 years, that history has been largely forgotten in our alarm over the Christian right. Yet it takes only a casual reading of major denominational teachings to see just how consistently progressive the faiths of millions of Americans remain—especially when compared to Democratic Party platforms, policies, and presidents in the last 30 years.

Here, for example, is an excerpt on "The Economic Community," from the core faith teachings of the 10-million-member United Methodist Church, the largest of America's mainline Protestant denominations:

> We claim all economic systems to be under the judgment of God no less than other facets of the created order. Therefore,

125

we recognize the responsibility of governments to develop and implement sound fiscal and monetary policies that provide for the economic life of individuals and corporate entities, and that ensure full employment and adequate incomes with a minimum of inflation. We believe private and public enterprises are responsible for the social costs of doing business, such as employment and environment pollution, and that they should be held accountable for these costs. We support measures that would reduce the concentration of wealth in the hands of a few. We further support efforts to revise tax structures and eliminate governmental support that now benefit the wealthy at the expense of other persons.

The document goes on to call for limits on the rights of private property, support for collective bargaining, the advancement of more meaningful work and leisure, and an end to the celebration of consumerism. It also endorses specific measures to help migrant labor, limit gambling, break up corporate monopolies, and increase various forms of "worksharing" and decentralized management on the job.

Or consider recent statements by the Presbyterian Church U.S.A., addressed to its three million members. The church's 1996 General Assembly sought, as one commentator put it, "nothing less than a full-scale assault on poverty at home and abroad, endorsing the provision of national health care, increases in the minimum wage and job-training programs, more investment in housing and education, an increase in U.S. international aid, and the development of a comprehensive plan to revive city life in the United States.". . .

The 2.5-million-member Episcopal Church is as explicitly unconservative as its larger Methodist and Presbyterian brethren, in some cases even more so. Its most recent national convention, for example, condemned Clinton's welfare reforms, urged new public support for migrant laborers, pressed for strict gun control and the abolition of nuclear weapons, and called for a new trial for Philadelphia death-row prisoner Mumia Abu-Jamal. It also committed the church to supporting local "living-wage" campaigns and launched a comprehensive study of "the theology of work" to begin redressing not only the material but also the moral and civic inequalities that have emerged in the past three decades.

The 60-million-member Catholic Church—its stance on

gender and abortion notwithstanding—is no less progressive than these mainline Protestant denominations on a host of social and political issues. The U.S. bishops' pastoral letter "Economic Justice for All," written in 1990, for example, is still a benchmark statement. More recently, the Catholic Church was the leader among the religious groups that fought Clinton's welfare reform bill and was deeply critical of its implications for social justice generally.

Millions of Americans are committed to these progressive organizations or to others that in social teachings are like them (the United Church of Christ, American Baptists, evangelical Lutherans, and several black Baptist and Methodist denominations as well as the smaller Unitarians, Quakers, and Reform Jews). Yet perhaps the most intriguing feature of this entire progressive wing of American religion is its invisibility to those not part of it.

Why the Invisibility?

The reasons for that invisibility aren't always easy to disentangle. Partly it has had to do with the increasing postwar secularization of the nation's elites, both in the universities and the press. One study of the elite Washington press corps, for example, found that 86 percent seldom or never attended religious services.

Equally important has been the mental redrawing of the important identity coordinates in American life, especially since the 1960s. Religious affiliation (in particular, denomination) historically served as a distinctive marker of one's location in America's social structure, as documented most famously by H. Richard Niebuhr's *Social Sources of Denominationalism*.

After World War II, a new spirit of ecumenism and the softening of denominational and religious borders—most celebrated in Will Herberg's 1950s classic *Protestant, Catholic, Jew*—set the stage for what Sydney Ahlstrom, in his Pulitzer Prize–winning history of American religion, has called the "coming of post-Protestant America."

In this world, especially since the 1960s, gender, race, and sexual preference have taken on new defining importance—and have powerfully submerged the older coordinates of religion, ethnicity, region, and class. Redressing the inequalities associated with the newly ascendant categories has become the defining mission of liberals and progressives alike.

Misreading the Religious Right

Ever since the rise of, first, Jerry Falwell and his Moral Majority in 1979 and, then, Pat Robertson and the Christian Coalition, many liberals, in their ignorance, have assumed American religion in general has turned conservative. Why, some have argued, haven't religious progressives created their own version of the Christian Coalition? It's a question that misreads what the Christian right has (and hasn't) accomplished—and why.

First, the secular changes of the twentieth century—especially in the years since World War II—have deeply threatened fundamentalists but have had no parallel effect on the liberal denominations. Fundamentalist Protestants draw on a belief in Biblical inerrancy, the emotional reality of imminent salvation, and a deep-seated suspicion of science and government because they compete with religion for authority. All these views, though, are generally alien to mainline Protestant, Jewish, and, in somewhat different ways, Catholic belief.

Second, religious progressives have long engaged the political system. As Princeton sociologist Robert Wuthnow and others have repeatedly found, mainline Protestants and Jews, for example, are typically twice as likely as fundamentalists to donate to a party, speak publicly on civic matters, serve in some public leadership role, or belong to politically engaged nonprofit groups.

There's another issue when it comes to replicating the presumed success of the religious right. Recent polling research suggests that rather than generating a dramatic rise in the ranks of religious conservatives, it is more likely that the Christian right found itself in effect free-riding as traditionally conservative southern voters became Republicans—a realignment that owed more to the civil-rights positions of Lyndon Johnson and Martin Luther King, Jr., than to the organizing abilities of Jerry Falwell and Pat Robertson.

Importantly, recent press accounts of the Christian right's viability suggest it is facing real—potentially fatal—problems after a 20-year run. As a *New York Times* article on the Christian Coalition reported in the summer of 1999,

> The coalition is hobbled by a $2.5 million debt, the departure of most of its experienced leaders and so much turnover in local leadership that it has strong affiliates in no more than 7 states, down from the 48 it claimed in 1998, according to its staff.

> And now even its prior assertions to such widespread strength are in doubt. Former national leaders . . . said in interviews that the coalition, as critics have long suspected, never commanded the numbers it claimed. . . .

> The coalition, these former leaders say, distorted the size of its base by keeping thousands of names of dead people, wrong addresses, and duplicates on its list of supporters; printed millions of voter guides that the coalition leaders expected would never be distributed, and hired temporary crews to look busy in the mail room and phone banks to impress reporters and camera crews.

> "We never distributed 40 million guides," says Dave Welch, the coalition's former national field director. "State affiliates took stacks of them to recycling centers after the election. . . ."

People can reasonably disagree about whether the whole Christian-right phenomenon has peaked and is now in decline—or has merely gone underground to focus on state and local politics, as some believe. It's worth noting, though, that both Paul Weyrich and Cal Thomas—major figures in the movement—now argue publicly that, in fact, the Christian right's two decades of efforts have "failed" and the time has come for its supporters to refocus primary attention instead on traditional evangelical concerns.

Committed and Caring People

Meanwhile, America's progressive religious community goes on—for the most part ignored by those who like to think of themselves as progressive but who have no connection to the nation's religious world. Of course, one can't count all the members or leaders of these churches and synagogues as avid supporters of their denominations' official views—far from it. In truth, like the Democratic Party or any labor union, progressive religion finds that large numbers of its constituents are indifferent, even sometimes hostile, to the voices of their leaders.

Yet the central fact remains: In an era when progressive voices seem few in number, when many progressive organizations struggle to meet payrolls, let alone advance agendas, America's progressive religious world represents a large body of committed and caring human beings—deeply bound, out of their own understanding of the connection between justice and the divine—who seek a world most of us could generously affirm. Like the rest of us, they struggle with their own limitations, their own internal conflicts and weaknesses. Yet time and again at crucial moments in American history, these same communities have risen up to resist abuses of human dignity and justice in the world around them.

*"[Conservative] evangelicals in the United
States are the largest identifiable group
that still believes in the American
experiment in ordered liberty."*

Religious Conservatism
Benefits Society

John Bolt

In the following viewpoint, John Bolt argues that those who
intend to maintain America's constitutional liberties should
adhere to religious conservatism rather than liberalism or
secularism. The nation's current cultural war is largely between progressive liberals—those who believe in rationalism
and subjective definitions of reality—and orthodox conservatives—those who believe in absolute truth and a transcendent authority. Bolt contends that while progressives champion political correctness, revisionist history, and revolutions
that often lead to violence, religious conservatives share a
common moral worldview and a belief in unchanging truths
that safeguard genuine freedom. Religious conservatives
should therefore be willing to engage in political and cultural battles to preserve liberty. Bolt is professor of system-
atic theology at Calvin Theological Seminary.

As you read, consider the following questions:

1. According to Bolt, in what ways do recent controversies
   over public education illustrate the cultural divide?
2. Why did Ed Dobson and Cal Thomas object to
   conservative evangelicals' involvement in American
   politics, according to the author?

I s putting on the battle fatigues of public warriors a fitting garb for Christians in America today? Does our situation require it or does Christian culture warfare bring scandal to the Gospel of the Prince of Peace? Do we want to be cast in the role of an "extremist" or "hate-monger"? Would our witness to our Lord and his kingdom of love not be strengthened by a principled renunciation of warfare rhetoric and tactics in the public square? Would that not contribute to much-needed civility in public discourse? These questions are being raised in the American evangelical world by such influential leaders as those two former foot-soldiers in the Religious Right, columnist Cal Thomas and Pastor Ed Dobson. Answers range from a denial that there is a real culture war—it's all a misunderstanding—to acknowledging that there is one but that it is a serious mistake for Christians to join it or promote it; that in fact Christians ought to be conscientious objectors to the culture wars.

The culture wars are unavoidable for Christians but we need to do some serious reflection on *how* to conduct them. There are ways of engaging these skirmishes so that the end result is not exclusion, division and oppression but rather inclusion and increased liberty. I believe that resisting the naysayers and culture war pacifists is important *for the sake of liberty*. If there is a deeper concern underlying everything I say today it is summed up by the words of Robert George printed on the back cover of Matthew Rose's essay on John Witherspoon.[1]

> I can see no more pressing need today than that which Witherspoon himself addressed two centuries ago—the training of young Christians to take their religiously-inspired convictions into the public square, there to contend for the allegiance of their fellow citizens on important matters of public policy.

I quite agree with Abraham Kuyper[2] who gave as reason for that same point the following: "There is not a square inch in the whole domain of our human existence over which Christ, who is Sovereign over *all*, does not cry: 'Mine!'". . .

1. Presbyterian minister John Witherspoon was the only clergyman to sign the Declaration of Independence. He believed that religious faith was essential in fostering true liberty.   2. Abraham Kuyper was the Dutch prime minister from 1901 to 1905. He believed that constitutional liberties were rooted in Calvinism.

Should Christians be warriors? Does the use of martial imagery, such as the endorsement of "culture wars" language, by itself contribute to a hostile environment in the public square? Does thinking in battle terms ("under attack or siege," "engaging the enemy"), and using such language in public, contribute to what Deborah Tannen has labeled "the argument culture" and thus undermine key goals of the Christian gospel such as reconciliation? More specifically, in view of the growing lament about the increasing lack of civility in American public life, does militancy of any sort—even if only rhetorical—not fuel the fires of uncivility and contribute to the coarsening of our public discourse? Is it not time for Christians to accept a cease fire in the culture wars, before the heated rhetoric moves from shouting to shooting? Let's consider some of the opponents of Christian participation in culture wars, the culture war pacifists, and why they are making their case. But first some definitions.

The Division in American Religion

Already in 1988, Princeton University sociologist Robert Wuthnow called attention to the realignment in American religion. On the basis of extensive surveys Wuthnow concluded that there existed "a deep division in American Religion: a division between self-styled religious 'conservatives' and self-styled religious 'liberals,' both of whom acknowledged a considerable tension with the other side." Wuthnow's analysis received further elaboration by James Davison Hunter in his 1991 book, *Culture Wars: The Struggle to Define America*. Hunter defines "cultural conflict very simply as political and social hostility rooted in different systems of moral understanding." He adds, "the end to which these hostilities tend is the domination of one cultural and moral ethos over all others." The core of this conflict, according to Hunter, can be traced ultimately to "the matter of moral authority . . . the basis by which people determine whether something is good or bad, right or wrong, acceptable or unacceptable."

Hunter insists that the current cultural conflict differs from previous skirmishes in American religious and cultural life (such as those between Protestants and Catholics as well as the conflicts between different varieties of Protestantism such as the "fundamentalist"/"modernist" conflict of the 1910s and 1920s). The key conflicts no longer take place "within the boundaries of a larger biblical culture—among numerous Protestant groups, Catholics, and Jews—over such issues as doctrine, ritual observance, and religious organization." These earlier conflicts were characterized by a common framework in which there "were basic agreements about the order of life in community and nation—agreements forged by biblical symbols and imagery." In other words, previous cultural conflicts took place within an agreed upon national mythology—a form of civil religion, if you will—and the disagreements had to do with theological and ecclesiastical matters revolving "around specific doctrinal issues or styles of religious practice and organization." That has changed. Today the very foundation is up for debate, "our most fundamental and cherished assumptions about how to order our lives—our own lives and our lives together in this society." Concludes Hunter, "our most fundamental ideas about who we are as Americans are now at odds." The new conflict, rooted in commitments "to different and opposing bases of moral authority and the world views that derive from them" . . . has created a cleavage in American life that "is so deep that it cuts across the old lines of conflict, making the distinctions that long divided Americans—those between Protestants, Catholics, and Jews—virtually irrelevant."

Hunter emphasizes that "though competing moral visions are at the heart of today's culture war, these do not always take form in coherent, clearly articulated, sharply differentiated world views." Instead, Hunter speaks of two *polarizing impulses* or *tendencies* in American culture." He contends that "the cleavages at the heart of the contemporary culture wars are created by . . . *the impulse toward orthodoxy* and *the impulse toward progressivism.*" The impulse toward orthodoxy he describes as "*the commitment on the part of adherents to an external, definable, and transcendent authority,*" whereas the progressivist impulse tends to define moral authority "by the spirit of the modern age, a spirit of rationalism and subjectivism." For those progressives that still "identify with a particular religious heritage," this impulse is characterized by *"the tendency to resymbolize historical faiths to the prevailing assumptions of contemporary life."* According to Hunter, these conflicting impulses cut across old divisions (Protestant, Catholic, Jew) joining liberals and conservatives respectively from the three traditions together in opposition to co-religionists of opposite views. This affects the entire range of North American public life—family, education, law, the media, and of course politics. That the public schools play a significant role in this culture war is not a matter of contention; both sides in the dispute agree on this point. On the one side, Hunter cites an opponent of "censorship" in public education who says,

> This country is experiencing a religious crusade as fierce as any out of the Middle Ages. . . . Our children are being sacrificed because of the fanatical zeal of our fundamentalist brothers who claim to be hearing the voice of God. . . . In this religious war, spiced with overtones of race and class, the books are an accessible target.

Similarly, the liberal activist group, People for the American Way, opposes all Internet filtering in public libraries and schools, as a violation of the First Amendment. From the opposing point of view, a spokesman for the National Association of Christian Educators claims:

> There is a great war waged in America . . . for the heart and mind and soul of every man, woman, and especially child in America. The combatants are 'secular humanism' and Christianity. Atheism, in the cloak of an acceptable 'humanitarian' religious philosophy, has been subtly introduced into the traditional Christian American culture through the public school system. The battle is for the minds of our youth.

In addition to the Family Research Council, a number of organizations were created specifically out of concern for the decline of American families (and marriages). Using the language of culture wars we hear talk of "an assault on the family." On the other side is the proliferation of bumper stickers that target the "family values" language used by many conservative evangelicals: "Hatred is not a family value."

The importance of the family and education is agreed to by both sides. Furthermore, both sides see the conflict about the family as a battle for the very soul of America and the future well-being of American society. James Dobson, founder of Focus on the Family, repeatedly speaks of the battle for the family as one for the health of the American *res publica*, and his most severe critics in turn have described his work as an attack on America itself. Barry Lynn, Executive Director of Americans United for the Separation of Church and State, contends, "James Dobson and Focus on the Family represent the greatest threat to constitutional liberties in our time." The high-pitched rhetoric is an indication of how high the stakes are regarded by both poles of the cultural divide. The battle is for America's soul.

Should Christians Avoid Political Conflict?

Ed Dobson and Cal Thomas, who co-authored *Blinded by Might: Why the Religious Right Can't Save America*, worked for Jerry Falwell during the glory days of the Moral Majority. The basic affirmation of *Blinded by Might* is that conservative, evangelical Christians, concerned about the social pathologies and moral dysfunctions of American life erred greatly when they embraced a *political* solution. The authors acknowledge "once believing that we could make things right through the manipulation of the political system." This was bound to fail because when it comes to politics, most evangelicals "are in unfamiliar territory" and furthermore, if we rely "mainly on politics to deliver us, we will never get that right because politics and government cannot reach into the soul. That is something God reserves for himself." . . .

But should Christians running for political office shed their identity as believers, or, as Attorney-General John Ashcroft's opponents would have it, discard their identity once in office? . . .

My point here is to make a distinction and raise a question. Yes, the purpose of politics should not be confused with the church's evangelizing, worshiping, discipling mission, but what is wrong with a separate and distinct political activity by Christian citizens? On any number of important issues many American evangelical Christians confuse the necessity of public civility with avoiding political conflict and mistakenly believe that developing personal relationships through friendship and witnessing is able to solve *political* conflict. Stated theologically, both ecclesiology [doctrine of the church] and public theology are underdeveloped in the evangelical world. . . . Is turning the cheek the way to respond to those who publicly compare supporting educational vouchers[3] with Fascism? Or does it require a different response, a political one? Should Christian citizens not resort to legal means when their First Amendment constitutional liberties are denied? When facing structural political or legal problems free citizens of a constitutionally lawful society have both a right and a responsibility to act politically. Is it possible or responsible today to be a believing Christian and a conscientious objector to the culture wars? . . .

"For the Glory of Our God"

I [now allude] to Kuyper the journalist, the founder and long-time editor of a Christian daily newspaper *De Standaard*. It was launched on April 1, 1872, the three-hundredth anniversary of the Sea Beggars' successful recapture of the Dutch port of Brill (Briel) from Spanish troops. As the nation was poised to celebrate the day of its liberation, Kuyper's lead editorial quoted William of Orange's plea to Dutch citizens that they give God glory for his providential guidance and in gratitude set aside personal ambition for the good of the nation. Then Kuyper applied the significance of the day to his own cause. He noted that his marginalized band of true believers and committed Calvinists was small but exulted,

> The fleet of the Sea Beggars was also small! The calling of [our small band] is so glorious! To engage in battle, not only for oneself and one's children, but also for one's fellow citizens, even for Europe, for humanity—so that *Justice* remains, *freedom of conscience* is not smothered, and the Prince's rallying cry once again rings true: "for the glory of our God."

Biblical imagery and national mythology in a martial mode in the service of a contemporary political cause is not unfamiliar to us. Martin Luther King Jr. made similar appeals to biblical imagery, to the founders, to Lincoln and so did President Reagan, both men effectively.

---

3. School vouchers enable parents to use state funds to send their children to private or religious schools.

Liberty Is at Stake

Almost everything I want to plead for was summarized in the last two paragraphs. Effective political mobilization requires a foundation of political imagination and vision. Think about it. In what year did the Moral Majority succeed best in getting its message through to the American people? A good case can be made that it was 1976, the "year of the evangelical" according to *Time* magazine which was America's bicentennial year and the juxtaposition of these two is not accidental. Evangelicals in the United States are the largest identifiable group that still believes in the American experiment in ordered liberty. The mainstream dominant culture with its revisionist historiography and multi-cultural political correctness believes that America is evil to its core, created and ruled by a militaristic, racist, misogynist, homophobic cabal of white European males. If a more conservative vision of America, a free America, is to be restored, it will require, I believe, a more creative, imaginative appeal to the American ideal of liberty. . . .

A Simple Faith

What kind of America *do* religious conservatives believe in? It is a nation of safe streets, strong families, schools that work, and marriages that stay together, one with a smaller government, lower taxes, and civil rights for all. Most religious conservatives do not countenance discrimination—or special rights—for anyone. Our faith is simple, and our agenda is direct.

For either political party to attack persons holding these views as "fanatics," "extremists," or worse violates a basic American spirit of fairness. More than that, it runs counter to all we are as a nation and all we aspire to be as a people.

Ralph Reed, *USA Today Magazine*, July 1997.

To pick up another theme from the last two paragraphs of the previous section, Kuyper's visionary sense might sound grandiose—for the Dutch nation, for Europe, for humanity—but his point that our passion for liberty is not in the first place for our own benefit needs to be underscored. I do believe there is a culture war in America today and that our liberty is at stake. I do not have time to prove it to you but ask yourself whether the suppression of dissent under the guise of hate speech, the attacks on the Boy Scouts of America, or the heated opposition to a voluntary Bible study in the office of the nation's attorney-general, are not symptomatic of efforts to suppress the freedom of religion guaranteed by the First Amendment. As the horror stories of such suppression increase (and they are increasing!), and the examples of public bigotry against evangelicals and Roman Catholics multiply, it becomes harder and harder to deny that there is a war going on. . . .

Genuine Religious Tolerance

[There] is a Jewish voice joining the chorus [for religious conservatism]. Daniel Lapin is a devout Orthodox Jewish rabbi who is convinced that America's Christian religious tradition does not, as secularists so often claim, represent "primitive tribalism and intolerance" but is rather America's only hope for survival. The "tug-of-war going on for the future of our country," he contends, "is whether America is a secular or religious nation." Defending a version of Christian America does not mean, according to Rabbi Lapin, "that Jews ought to embrace the Christian faith. I believe that all Jews should actively embrace traditional Judaism; I have spent many years of my life helping to bring that about." Nonetheless, he adds,

> I am suggesting, at the very least, that Jews should stop speaking and acting as if Christian America is their enemy. I feel that all Americans who love freedom, whether or not they are religious, should be reassured, not frightened, by the reawakening of earnest Christianity throughout the land. I shall try to establish that Jews as well as other minorities have the most to fear from a *post*-Christian America.

Stated differently, the hope for genuine religious tolerance in America, for pluralism, is in recovering a common Christian moral vision. Conversely, contrary to much conventional wisdom, secularism is a *threat* to tolerance and pluralism. In Rabbi Lapin's words, "the choice is between a benign Christian culture and a sinister secular one." In *Christianity Today*, Daniel Taylor prods us to reconsider the nature of tolerance:

First, one is not tolerant of something unless one objects to it. I do not tolerate something I either accept or am indifferent to, because it requires nothing of me. Most social liberals, for instance, cannot rightfully be said to be tolerant regarding homosexual behavior since they have no objection to it. You do not have to tolerate that which you accept or affirm.

Taylor then posits the same counter-intuitive proposition we have already encountered: Religious conservatives may be more tolerant than progressive liberals:

> If tolerance requires an initial objection, then conservatives, ironically, may be much more tolerant than liberals, because there are so many more things to which they object. The least tolerant person is the person who accepts everything, because such a person is not required to overcome any internal objections. To paraphrase G.K. Chesterton, turnips are singularly tolerant.

The paradox is that tolerance requires holding definite views and being willing to sacrifice. We only "tolerate" that of which we disapprove. To be tolerant is, paradoxically, in a certain way to be intolerant. One objects to certain ideas but, within certain limits, voluntarily withholds use of coercive power in an effort to tolerate publicly what one finds objectionable personally.

A Reality in American Life

The problem with Rabbi Lapin's judgment that a "benign Christian culture" is to be preferred to a sinister, secular one, is that radical church-state separatists judge the very idea of a Christian culture itself to be necessarily sinister. Joining secularists, in a perfect illustration of James Hunter's thesis, the April 6, 1999 newsletter of the Baptist Joint Committee referred to the "darker dimension" of the "demons that push the drive for [school] vouchers," calling this particular initiative "selfish . . . parochial . . . greedy . . . racist." For good measure a reference to "Hitler's grand schemes" was also thrown in. In such instances, those with whom we disagree are not merely persons with different viewpoints, not even persons with *dumb* views, but *evil* people with *evil* ideas. We demonize the *other*. The logical consequence of such demonization is the desire not simply to cast ideas into disrepute by discrediting them with good arguments and persuasive rhetoric, but ultimately to eliminate the people who hold the views. Thankfully not all who use the rhetoric of demonization follow their beliefs through to the logical end but there can be little doubt that the rhetoric of demonization thoroughly poisons the public square and makes a civil society practically impossible. . . .

The active public role of religion results in freedom; secularism leads to tyranny. The struggle for freedom of religious expression at the heart of the culture wars is the cornerstone of a larger battle for liberty. Deliberately abstaining from the culture wars is thus an abstinence from the battle for liberty.

The culture wars are a reality of American life and they reflect an important debate about the very nature and future of the American experiment in ordered liberty. Perhaps the question about the culture wars comes down to this: Is this essentially a battle about liberty? The degree to which we are willing to participate in the culture wars may come down to a decision about that question. If the battle is only about differences in politics, about specifics of government policy, it is important for Christians to back off from the fierceness that has characterized much of the culture wars rhetoric in recent years. But what if the culture wars are really about our fundamental liberties? Conflict about liberty cannot be a trifling or indifferent matter for Christians. History shows clearly that genuine liberty is both precious and fragile. The memory of those who died to establish, defend, and preserve the liberty we enjoy must not be dishonored by our unwillingness to engage in cultural and political combat for the same liberty. The fight for liberty is one in which we ought to be willing to engage.

But how? Since culture is the foundation of politics, religious conservatives need to encourage the development of an alternative imagination to that of secular modernity. . . . The imagination of modernity is escapist. Moderns set aside the notion of sin and its correlative notion of limits. The good life, a happy life, without pain, toil or trouble, is understood as a *right* and our failure to enjoy such a life must be due to oppressive, alienating structures and institutions. After all doesn't it say somewhere that happiness is one of those "self-evident" and "inalienable rights" along with life and liberty? If we are unhappy we must conclude that our crummy lot in life is a result of victimization by these structures. In our oppressed state we begin to daydream about how it ought to be and "daydream becomes the vantage point from which to judge existence." Salvation comes through liberation from these structures by means of revolutionary change. From this romantic-utopian daydreaming it is, as the twentieth century has shown, only a few steps to violence engaged to remove the obstacle to fulfill our utopian longings, be they Czars, Ukranian peasants, Jews, or whoever.

The proper response to this, according to Claes Ryn, is not to suppress the imagination of romantic escape in favor of reason (the solution of Plato and Locke) but to renew it in a realistic, non-escapist direction. Such art must direct us beyond ourselves and our wishes to the kind of moral imagination that underscores the permanent things.

> *"Humanism advocates a richly rewarding,*
> *ethical way of life based on empathic,*
> *compassionate caring about others' needs,*
> *not on obedience to imagined divine*
> *authority."*

Secular Humanism Should Be Promoted

Robert F. Morse

The guiding principles of humanism are rooted in intellect, science, critical thinking, and experience rather than belief in divine authority, writes Robert F. Morse in the following viewpoint. Humanistic values are based on compassion, enlightened judgment, and respect for human dignity and needs, he explains. Humanism's regard for empathy, reasoned discussion, and human rights has actually helped religion to evolve out of its tendency toward narrow-mindedness and barbarism. The author concludes that humanists and liberal religious believers should work together to improve life on earth. Morse is vice president of the Humanists of Broward County, Florida.

As you read, consider the following questions:

1. According to Morse, what are the four general principles of humanism?
2. What do religious believers' opinions about God actually reveal, in the author's opinion?
3. In the author's opinion, what is dangerous about fundamentalist religious belief and fundamentalist atheism?

Robert F. Morse, "Humanism: One Activist's View," *Free Inquiry*, vol. 21, Fall 2001, p. 22. Copyright © 2001 by *Free Inquiry*. Reproduced by permission.

People come to humanism from many starting points; mine is only one perspective. Humanism has no single arbiter or creed. Humanist thought has evolved throughout history in step with humankind's evolving knowledge about reality. I believe this evolution has reflected four general principles.

1. Humanism is a philosophy and guide to living for people who think for themselves. It is consistent with what we know about reality and is based on reason, science, human experience, and critical thinking. People of reason rather than faith, we weigh even religious claims against our own judgment and experience, infuriating would-be arbiters of divine authority.

2. Humanism advocates a richly rewarding, ethical way of life based on empathic, compassionate caring about others' needs, not on obedience to imagined divine authority. We consider the Golden Rule a basic ethical guide.

3. Humanism respects human dignity and possibilities. We do not see ourselves as "children of God who can never grow up" or as chattels of God—we are not "clay for the Potter," as Paul argued in Romans 9:20–23. We value every human's feelings, wants, needs, empathy, compassion, intellect, and aspirations.

4. Humanists try to be in tune with enlightened social understandings. We are committed to human rights and to meeting the basic needs of all people; to civil liberties, church-state separation, participatory democracy, the expansion of global consciousness, and to the needs of the environment and of posterity.

The Evolution of Reason

Like our understandings of reality, religious beliefs, too, evolved throughout human existence. We think the continued evolution of these understandings and beliefs—aided by reason, free inquiry, and open discussion—is generally beneficial and should be encouraged. We think "evolution" reflects reality more accurately than "creationism," and that reason and critical thinking yield better understandings of reality than the purported revelations of ancient scriptures. Still, we who champion science make no claims to transcendent knowledge. Every principle of humanism is a scientific hypothesis, as consistent with the preponderance of known evidence as can be, but—unlike articles of faith—always subject to being disconfirmed by new knowledge.

In contrast, religious believers often differ about the "will" and characteristics they attribute to God. Proponents characteristically put their own preferences into God's mouth to justify their own predilections. Or they attribute mutually contradictory characteristics to the God of their imaginings. There seems to be no reliable standard for deciding between their conflicting claims. What individuals declare about their God reveals far less about divine reality than it does about the speaker.

Tomorrow. © 2002 by Dan Perkins. Reprinted with permission.

Humanists care more about persons' behavior than their beliefs. Thus, many of us welcome caring, liberal persons into the humanist community and seek to work with them for the betterment of life on Earth. Most nonfundamentalist or "liberal" religious believers agree with basic humanist principles and share many of our humanist values. There is nothing basic to "generic humanism" about which liberal religious believers need object.

Humanist Naturalists

A subset among humanists are impressed that every phenomenon scientists have learned to understand seems to rely on natural causes alone. Extrapolating from this, they conclude that *all* things have probably *always* occurred through natural causes alone. Such "humanist naturalists" are unaware of any credible evidence for an immaterial soul, a life after earthly death, or a supernatural deity. But they can no more *prove* these conclusions than religious believers can *prove* theirs. Within the humanist community some "fundamentalist atheists" would reject anyone who is not an atheist, just as fundamentalist believers reject those whose worldviews do not precisely match their own. Fundamentalism from whatever quarter reflects emotional immaturity. It blunts the intellect and interferes with problem solving. Ultimately it erodes the willingness to cooperate that alone can make life on Earth more rewarding for us all.

Some believers might find this surprising, but it is the values we have already identified as foundational to humanism—consistency with reality, empathic compassion, respect for reason and the scientific method, and respect for the needs and dignity of human beings—that have encouraged religions to evolve out of primitive barbarity. Religion is a powerful motivator. Among good, caring people, and leavened by humanist values, faith can be constructive.

A Moral Compass

Neither belief nor nonbelief in a supernatural deity conduces automatically to goodness. Indeed, religion is very much a two-edged sword. It has been invoked to justify wars, crusades, hatred, the slaughter of dissenters, human sacrifice, terrorism, slavery, the subjugation of women and children, violations of human rights, the disparagement of sexuality, and today's disastrous overpopulation, among many other evils. It seems abundantly clear that, without foundational humanist values to mellow, guide, and restrain it, religion can become too dangerous to have around.

Humanism has always been the "moral compass" guiding religion toward decency. Is it not the implicit humanism expressed by figures like Confucius, Buddha, Amos and Micah, Jesus, Abraham Lincoln, Mohandas Gandhi, Eleanor Roosevelt, and Martin Luther King that has led persons of all persuasions the world over to respect and revere them?

Where religion has been "leavened" by the foundational values of humanism, humanists should not hesitate to make common cause with believers regarding the concerns they share.

> "Will we model a life that honors God by obeying His Word, or by our choices will we side with the humanist lie that each of us decides for ourselves what is right and wrong?"

Secular Humanism Is Harmful

Tim LaHaye

In the following viewpoint, Tim LaHaye argues that secular humanism is a dangerous worldview that exalts man's knowledge rather than God's wisdom. This atheistic and amoral philosophy has infiltrated government, education, and popular culture, and is currently causing a moral decline in the United States and the Western world, contends LaHaye. He maintains that reversing the damage caused by secular humanism will require Bible-believing Christians to pray, become politically active, and educate themselves and others about current events. LaHaye, a conservative evangelical Christian minister and educator, is coauthor of the *Left Behind* fiction series.

As you read, consider the following questions:
1. In LaHaye's opinion, what five major tenets is secular humanism based on?
2. What are some of humanism's buzzwords, according to LaHaye?
3. In the author's view, what should "pro-moral" activists do to reverse the nation's moral decline?

Tim LaHaye, "The Battle for Your Mind," *Moody*, vol. 101, January/February 2001, pp. 32–33. Copyright © 2001 by Tim LaHaye. Reproduced by permission.

Throughout your life you face a battle for your mind: whether you will live by man's wisdom or God's (1 Cor. 1:17–25). Man's wisdom has taken the multifaceted form of secular humanism, while God's wisdom is revealed in the Bible and displayed throughout His creation (Prov. 3:19; Jer. 51:15). Which of these two options you choose will affect the way you live now and ultimately where you will spend eternity.

The Threat

Secular humanism is an anti-God world-view built on five major tenets: atheism, evolution, amorality, human autonomy, and globalism. More people, including believers, are being adversely affected by secularist thinking than we often realize. It dominates the Western world, having captured education, government, law, medicine, psychology, sociology, the arts, business, TV, publications, movies, and radio.

Just consider a few of its buzzwords: *global security; world citizenship; democratic socialism; progressive constitutionalism; no-fault divorce; tolerance; gay theology; partial-birth abortion; homophobic; vast right-wing conspiracy.* The list seems endless.

Some readers might say, "None of that stuff concerns me." Yet if you are a Christian, this is your fight. Every day you and I must choose between humanist or biblical paths:

• Will we model a life that honors God by obeying His Word, or by our choices will we side with the humanist lie that each of us decides for ourselves what is right and wrong?

• Will we bring all our financial decisions to God in prayer, or will we swallow humanism's atheistic lie and act as if there were no God?

• Will we monitor and discuss what our children are learning in biology class, or will we abandon them to the evolutionary lies of secular humanism?

• Will we teach our sons and daughters that sexual intercourse is a gift from God, to be enjoyed only within marriage, or by our silence will we endorse the humanist lie that sexual expression is just a matter of preference?

• Will we in the United States encourage our children to be true patriots, grateful for our Christian heritage and willing to uphold its founding precepts, or will we passively accept the nation's slide toward godlessness?

Believe me, this is no armchair debate—especially if you love your children. Did you know that secular humanism especially focuses on attacking our youth? The battle for the mind that is now raging looks much as it did in New Testament days. It remains the same battle between good and evil.

The Same Old Lie

Secular humanism is really little more than a repackaged version of the ancient satanic doctrine that ruined Eden. Remember how the devil convinced Eve to eat of the forbidden fruit? "You will be like God," the serpent hissed, "knowing good and evil" (Gen. 3:5). Ever since that fateful day, the unchanging goal of rebellious mankind has been to sit on God's throne. The Antichrist, the man the Bible pictures as the very embodiment of human rebellion, will first and foremost be a worshiper of himself (Dan. 1:36–37).

This epitome of secular humanism "will oppose and will exalt himself over everything that is called God or is worshiped, so that he sets himself up in God's temple, proclaiming himself to be God," says the apostle Paul (2 Thess. 2:4). In every age, this remains the temptation: to believe the devil's lie and to imagine that we have become God. This is I-dolatry at its ugly core, to exalt and magnify oneself above all gods—to set oneself up in the temple of one's mind as God.

The Christian must bring such debased ideas and beliefs to Christ for His light. Paul tells us in Romans 12:2 that we must not be conformed to this world, but be transformed by the renewing of our mind, that we may prove what is the good, acceptable, and perfect will of God.

Christians cannot remain neutral and forgo this battle for the heart and mind. Elijah took on the state religion of Baal and Ashtaroth at Mount Carmel (1 Kings 18). Jesus Christ took on the Greeks (Pan) and the Romans (Caesar) on a high mountain (Matt. 16, 17). Paul took on the Greek philosophers (Epicureans and Stoics) at Mars Hill (Acts 17). All engaged the battle. None raised the white flag to surrender.

We must do no less, else every idea that Christians hold dear, as well as the institutions based on these ideas—home, church, and state—will be lost.

Time for Action

In the 1940s my godly pastor echoed the unwise advice of many Christians when he taught, "Politics is a dirty business. Rather than getting involved in politics, we Christians should stick to preaching the gospel and let the nice civic-minded people run the country." I do not condemn him for this, for I acted with equal apathy during the '50s and '60s. Until then I had never recruited anyone for public office. Then, in the providence of God, I learned a painful lesson when our church attempted to get a zoning ordinance passed by the city council. After $200,000 and three years of effort, we lost, 6-2. For the first time, I realized that men and women largely hostile to the church controlled our city.

Varvel. © 1999 by *The Indianapolis Star*. Reprinted by permission of Creators Syndicate, Inc.

Gradually that has changed. Christians, with the backing of fellow believers throughout that city, have won elections, while others who value high morals have replaced humanists or those influenced by humanists. These pro-moral additions have helped to crack down on massage parlors and porn shops. Churches are now given a fair hearing for their growth needs.

Look around and you'll see we are in a cosmic war for the soul of our country. It takes armies to win wars. We need an army of pro-moral activists, encouraged by their Bible-believing ministers, who will provide America with the spiritual and moral leadership for which it yearns.

So what can we do? In my book *Mind Siege*, I develop at least 19 strategies that any of us can pursue. For now, let me suggest just a few:

First, if we are going to turn this country around, Christians must vote. We need more Christians to become responsible citizens by going to the polls and voting into office only those who share your moral values, regardless of the candidate's party affiliation.

Second, obey the command to believers in 1 Timothy 2:1–2 and pray for those in authority over you—the officials in your city, county, state, and nation. Ask the Lord to give them His wisdom that they might not be duped by the lies of secular humanism.

Third, read all you can about what's happening in your world and share your insights with friends and neighbors. Get informed! Don't allow the enemy to win simply by our ignorance.

Last, make sure that you don't gain the world but lose your soul (Matt. 16:26).We must do all we can to recapture the culture, but we can never lose sight of what's truly important. We are to "seek first the kingdom of God and His righteousness" (Matt. 6:33). Consider this a wake-up call for all evangelical Christians to:

- Herald Messiah's message (2 Cor. 5:18–20).
- Be lights in the world (Matt. 5:16; Phil. 2:15).
- Raise the moral climate of our culture (Matt. 5:13; 25:35; Jude 1:22; Col. 3:12–23; Rom. 12, 13, 14).

Defeating the Humanist Agenda

I believe we still have time to defeat the humanist agenda and to reverse America's moral decline. Our country does not have to remain on its current Sodom and Gomorrah course. I believe God will yet bless this nation and give us another great revival. It will come, however, only if we get serious about our Christian beliefs, aims, and actions.

You can decide, with God's help, to use whatever gifts, talents, and energy you possess to steer this country away from the rocks of secular humanism. Each one of us can be a lighthouse.

So let us be about our Father's business of protecting and defending our children (Matt. 18). Let us contend earnestly for the faith (Jude 1:3). Let us declare the gospel of Jesus Christ as Messiah and Lord (Rom. 1:3–17; 1 Cor. 15:1–4). Let us understand the times in which we live so we will know what to do (1 Chron. 12:32). Let us judge every idea by bringing it to Christ (2 Cor. 10:5). And let us not be deceived by vain and deceitful world-views (Col. 2:8). That should keep us occupied, challenged, satisfied, and living victoriously until our life is over or He comes for His family!

"[Multiculturalism] is part of a broader movement to create a more equitable society."

Multiculturalism Should Be Promoted

Part I: *Rethinking Schools*; Part II: James A. Banks

The authors of the following two-part viewpoint discuss the benefits and challenges of multiculturalism, a value system that cultivates respect for people from diverse racial, social, and cultural backgrounds. In Part I, the editors of *Rethinking Schools* define multiculturalism as part of the larger struggle against oppression based on ethnicity, gender, class, sexual orientation, and physical ability. Multicultural educators, they argue, actively confront discrimination and seek ways to foster economic and social justice. In Part II, James A. Banks contends that multicultural education gives students from various backgrounds the skills necessary to work in and contribute to a culturally diverse society. *Rethinking Schools* is a quarterly newspaper that advocates progressive public school reforms. Banks is director of the Center for Multicultural Education at the University of Washington in Seattle.

As you read, consider the following questions:

1. According to the editors of *Rethinking Schools*, how do multicultural perspectives enhance the study of history?
2. What percentage of students will be people of color in the year 2020, according to the editors?
3. In Banks's opinion, what is the aim of multicultural education?

I

Multiculturalism? "We did that back in the '80s," seems to be the attitude of many educational leaders these days. The birthday of Martin Luther King Jr. was included in the holiday pantheon, new textbooks were purchased, the most offensive materials discarded, ethnically-themed assemblies added, staff in-services held. Been there, done that.

This waning interest is in part the product of relentless haranguing by the right. The Lynne Cheneys and Rush Limbaughs slam multicultural education as divisive, Balkanizing, politically correct, ethnic cheerleading. These criticisms coincide with a broader offensive against people of color and people who are poor: the repeal of affirmative action, skyrocketing incarceration rates—especially of Black men, families kicked off welfare with no other supports in place, and jingoistic anti-immigrant initiatives.

And the proliferation of high stakes standardized testing has begun to strangle the life out of anything in school that can't promise to increase students' scores. Who has time for multicultural education when there are multiple choice tests to prepare for? Indeed, the push to subordinate teaching to state standards and tests is explicitly regarded by some as a means to eliminate multicultural education.

A Fight for Justice

What is multicultural education? At its best, multiculturalism is an ongoing process of questioning, revising, and struggling to create greater equity in every nook and cranny of school life—whether in curriculum materials, school staffing policies, discipline procedures, teaching strategies, or course offerings. And it is part of a broader movement to create a more equitable society. It is a fight against racism and other forms of oppression, including those based on class, gender, religion, sexual orientation, physical ability, or national origin and language. It is a fight for economic and social justice.

But this is not to say that multiculturalism is polemical or politically partisan in a narrow sense. In curriculum, for example, academic rigor is impossible without a multicultural standpoint. Suppose one is teaching about the American Revolution. Traditional—non-multicultural—curricular approaches to the revolution focus on the actions of Washington, Jefferson, Franklin and other "great men." But in 1776, the majority of people in the 13 colonies were women, African Americans, or Native Americans. They pursued their dreams in ways that profoundly impacted the revolution. For instance, when enslaved African Americans in the South discovered that the rhetoric of freedom excluded them, they fled in droves, dramatically influencing the course of the war, leading to what some scholars have called "the largest slave insurrection in American history." There is no way to make sense of events following the Declaration of Independence—or any other historical era—without a multicultural perspective.

Such a perspective is not simply about explaining society, it is about changing it. Multiculturalism interrogates the world from a critical and activist standpoint: Who benefits and who suffers from any particular arrangement? How can we make it more just? At a superficial level, multicultural education celebrates diversity. More deeply, it equips educators, students, and parents to recognize and critique how some differences lead to deficit and others to privilege. And it compels us to seek alternatives.

In the classroom, multiculturalism means examining teaching materials for bias and omission, but also requires that we ask hard questions of ourselves and our classrooms. Are all our students fairly served? Does our choice of lessons favor some students over others? Whose cultures are represented on the classroom's walls? Do our expectations of students differ based on race, ethnicity, nationality, class, or gender?

White Privilege

For white educators, pursuing a rigorous multiculturalism is especially important—and difficult. In society, those on top have the greatest difficulty recognizing their own dominance. Things seem fine to the comfortable. So those who are white need to assume the responsibility of questioning how white privilege plays out in every aspect of their educational lives. As anti-racist educator Enid Lee points out in *Rethinking Our Classrooms*, "Oftentimes, whatever is white is treated as normal. So when teachers choose literature that they say will deal with a universal theme or story, like childhood, all the people in the stories are of European origin; it's basically white culture and civilization. That culture is different from others, but it doesn't get named as different. It gets named as normal."

For white educators, a multicultural perspective means examining how racism has affected all aspects of one's identity and experiences. It also means dialoging with educators and parents of color and other oppressed groups in order to understand how school is not experienced the same by everyone.

The Origins of Multiculturalism

Multicultural education can be traced historically to the Civil Rights Movement. African-American scholars and educators, working in conjunction with the Civil Rights Movement as a whole, provided much of the leadership of multicultural education.

The term "multiethnic education" was used to bridge racial and ethnic groups: "multicultural education" broadened the umbrella to include gender and other forms of diversity. The term "culture" rather than "racism" was adopted mainly so that audiences of white educators would listen. As a result, however, many white educators have pulled multicultural education away from social struggles and redefined it to mean the celebration of ethnic foods and festivals; the field is sometimes criticized as having turned away from its initial critique of racism in education. It is important to locate multicultural education in the Civil Rights struggle for freedom, political power, and economic integration.

Christine Sleeter and Peter McLaren, *Rethinking Schools*, Fall 2000.

Lest we be discouraged by the requirements of multiculturalism, we should remind ourselves that multiculturalism is not merely an individual self-improvement project. Building a multicultural, anti-racist, pro-justice school culture is fundamentally a collective enterprise. It means working together. It means building partnerships between schools, curriculum departments, unions, parent groups, and social justice organizations. It means establishing ongoing inservice education for new and veteran teachers. It means that we demand the time and money necessary to rethink and reorient school life. Multiculturalism requires more than good intentions; it needs support.

It also requires room to grow. So it's essential to organize against those aspects of school "reform," like high-stakes standardized testing, that threaten to suffocate multicultural initiatives.

Schools may have retreated from an earlier enthusiasm for multiculturalism, but there are signs of hope. In a relatively short period, multicultural scholarship has become a powerful intellectual force on college campuses. Teacher education programs are increasing numbers of individuals exposed to issues of how race and culture play out in school contexts. And there have never been more high-quality multicultural teaching resources available to educators. Even demographic projections offer hope. As multicultural scholar James Banks notes . . . by 2020 it's estimated that the nation's schools will have 48% students of color. Although positive change will not automatically result from such population shifts, Banks suggests that schools may be more open to multicultural approaches if America's student body is more diverse.

We want our schools to be multicultural, anti-racist and pro-justice because we want the larger society to manifest those same values. To the greatest extent possible, schools and classrooms should work toward and exemplify the kind of society we hope to live in. We urge readers to renew their commitment to multicultural, anti-racist education as part of a broader struggle for a better world.

II

An important goal of multicultural education is to educate citizens who can participate successfully in the workforce and take action in the civic community to help the nation actualize its democratic ideals. These ideals, such as justice, equality and freedom, are set forth in the Declaration of Independence, the U.S. Constitution and the Bill of Rights.

Democratic societies, such as the United States, are works in progress that require citizens who are committed to democratic ideals, who are keenly aware of the gap between a nation's ideals and realities and who are able and willing to take thoughtful action that will help make democratic ideals a reality.

Although some critics have misrepresented multicultural

education and argued it is divisive and will Balkanize the nation, the aim of multicultural education is to unify our nation and to help put in place its ideal of *e pluribus unum*— "out of many, one."

The claim by conservative social commentators that multicultural education will divide the nation assumes that it is now united. However, our nation is deeply divided along racial, ethnic and social-class lines. Multicultural education is trying to help unify a deeply divided nation, not to divide one that is united.

Multicultural theorists assume that we cannot unite the nation around its democratic ideals by forcing people from different racial, ethnic and cultural groups to leave their cultures and languages at the schoolhouse door. An important principle of a democratic society is that citizens will voluntarily participate in the commonwealth and that their participation will enrich the nation-state.

When citizens participate in society and bring their cultural strengths to the national civic culture, both they and the nation are enriched. Renato Rosaldo, the Stanford anthropologist, calls this kind of civic participation *cultural citizenship*.

We can create an inclusive, democratic and civic national community only when we change the center to make it more inclusive and reflective of the diversity that enriches our nation. This will require that we bring people and groups that are now on the margins of society into the center.

Schools should be model communities that mirror the kind of democratic society we envision. In democratic schools the curriculum reflects the cultures of the diverse groups within society, the languages and dialects that students speak are respected and valued, cooperation rather than competition is fostered among students and students from diverse racial, ethnic and social-class groups are given equal status in the school. . . .

Too often multicultural education is conceptualized narrowly to mean adding content about diverse groups to the curriculum or expanding the canon taught in schools. It also should help students to develop more democratic racial and ethnic attitudes and to understand the cultural assumptions that underlie knowledge claims.

Another important dimension of multicultural education is equity pedagogy, in which teachers modify their teaching in ways that will facilitate the academic achievement of students from diverse racial, cultural, language and social-class groups.

What the Evidence Indicates

Educational leaders should become familiar with the research evidence about the effects of multicultural education and not be distracted by the critics of multicultural education who disregard or distort this significant body of research.

Research indicates that students come to school with many stereotypes, misconceptions and negative attitudes toward outside racial and ethnic groups. Research also indicates that the use of multicultural textbooks, other teaching materials and cooperative teaching strategies can help students to develop more positive racial attitudes and perceptions.

This research also indicates that these kinds of materials and teaching strategies can result in students choosing more friends from outside racial, ethnic and cultural groups. . . .

School leaders should recognize that the goals of multicultural education are highly consistent with those of the nation's schools: to develop thoughtful citizens who can function effectively in the world of work and in the civic community. Ways must be found for schools to recognize and respect the cultures and languages of students from diverse groups while at the same time working to develop an overarching national culture to which all groups will have allegiance.

This can best be done by bringing groups that are on the margins of society into the center, educating students who have the knowledge, skills and values needed to rethink and change the center so that it is more inclusive and incorporating the research and theory in multicultural education into school reform.

Rethinking and re-imaging our nation in ways that will make it more just and equitable will enrich us all because the fates of all groups are tightly interconnected. Martin Luther King Jr. said, "We will live together as brothers and sisters or die separate and apart as strangers."

"The aggressive promotion of the multicultural agenda [is] an assault on the academic enterprise."

Multiculturalism Is Harmful

Bradford P. Wilson

In the following viewpoint, Bradford P. Wilson argues that multiculturalism now permeates college campuses and is compromising the intellectual integrity of higher education. In a misguided attempt to embrace diversity, universities have adopted policies and programs that emphasize difference, including race and gender quotas, ethnic and gay and lesbian studies programs, segregated dormitories, and mandatory sensitivity training. An emphasis on radical feminism and the identity politics of oppressed groups encourages students to see the world only through the lens of race, class, and gender, Wilson contends. The result is student divisiveness, reduced academic rigor, increased complaints about victimization, and a lack of appreciation for genuine human diversity, he concludes. Wilson is the executive director of the National Association of Scholars in Princeton, New Jersey.

As you read, consider the following questions:

1. Why was a popular Arizona State University theater professor dismissed from his position in 1996, according to Wilson?
2. In the author's view, what cultures are not recognized in the academy's notion of diversity?
3. According to Wilson, how did the politicization of academic life begin?

Bradford P. Wilson, "The Culture Wars in Higher Education," *National Forum: The Phi Kappa Phi Journal*, vol. 79, Winter 1999, pp. 14–18. Copyright © 1999 by The Phi Kappa Phi Forum. Reproduced by permission.

As I write, I have before me recent higher-education news from *The Chronicle of Higher Education*. Last week, it informs me, seventy students (equal numbers of whites and blacks) occupied the office of the president of the University of New Hampshire [UNH], refusing to leave until certain demands had been met. These demands included "a more than fourfold increase in the number of black students, the recruitment of eighteen full-time black faculty members by 2005, and the creation of a mandatory prejudice-reduction workshop for all students, faculty members, and staff members." Within days, UNH had capitulated. The workshops begin in the fall of 2000.

At the University of Pennsylvania, a student yelled to a group of rowdy sorority sisters, "Shut up, you water buffalo!" and found himself in a Kafkaesque world of formal charges against him of racial harassment and an administration offering to make his troubles go away if only he would submit to public self-criticism and false confession, mandatory diversity training, residential probation, and a notation on his transcript of his having violated Penn's racial-harassment policy.

At Springfield College in Massachusetts, faculty were summoned to a faculty-development workshop with outside diversity consultants and, as one participant wrote, "I and other more senior colleagues were made to walk in a circle asking and answering pre-set questions and confessing to alleged 'secret racist predispositions' to perfect strangers."

In the fall semester of 1997, the women's studies program at the New Paltz campus of the State University of New York sponsored a conference titled "Revolting Behavior" which brought in sex-trade entrepreneurs to offer training in the huff-and-puff of lesbian sadomasochism and the use of sex toys. When New Paltz's president was asked to defend the academic merits of the workshops, he refused to exercise judgment. Instead, he invoked the time-honored principle of academic freedom, apparently conferring faculty-for-a-day status upon the owner of Eve's Garden in Manhattan and upon Shelly Mars, a "performance artist" who, in acting out various sadomasochistic sexual fantasies, drew upon her vast experience as a stripper in a bisexual bathhouse. For his part, the university's president soon thereafter received the American Association of University Professors' Alexander Meiklejohn Award for his "outstanding contribution to academic freedom."

In late 1996, the chairman of the theater department at Arizona State University dismissed a popular untenured theater professor from his teaching position because "the feminists are offended by the selection [sic] works from a sexist European canon that is approached traditionally." Translation? The hapless professor used plays from Shakespeare, Congreve, and Ibsen to train students in the art of performing. In firing him, his department head, as she wrote in a memo, was simply holding him accountable for failing to adopt "postmodern feminist/ethnic canons and production styles."

West Virginia University [WVU] left the job of writing a speech/ harassment code, applicable to faculty and students alike, to its Executive Officer for Social Justice. (Yes, the Mountaineers have an Office for Social Justice.) The draconian code was a mere reflection of the director's enlightened sensibilities, on display, for example, when she instructed all incoming tenure-track faculty in the fall of 1995 to avoid terms such as "boyfriend" and "girlfriend" in favor of terms such as "lover," "friend," and "partner." To err, a glance at WVU's code makes clear, would be to run afoul of the prohibition on heterosexism, resulting in sanctions "ranging from reprimand and warning to expulsion and termination, and including public service and educational remediation."

I begin with these few human-interest stories to give the reader, particularly one who has moved beyond his or her student days to a mature life beyond Alma Mater, a glimpse of the public ethos now regnant, or struggling for sovereignty, at all but the most culturally isolated American colleges and universities. Any doubts about the representative character of these illustrations will evaporate upon reading the meticulously documented book *The Shadow University: The Betrayal of Liberty on America's Campuses*, by Penn historian Alan Charles Kors and civil libertarian Harvey A. Silverglate.

The Contemporary Academic Climate
What ideas and sensibilities can we identify as guiding the contemporary academic climate hinted at in these examples?

Identity politics, radical feminism, multiculturalism, educating for difference, postmodernism, and deconstruction are, when taken together, perhaps sufficient to the purpose. . . .

A Divisive Principle

John O'Sullivan, editor of *National Review*, decries the multiculturalist assertion that America is an "idea rather than a nation [possessing] a distinctive but encompassing American identity." Peter W. Cookson, Jr., author of *School Choice: The Struggle for the Soul of American Education*, offers the insight that multiculturalism's hostility to the West and repudiation of an identifiable American culture is augmented by a radically new definition of community, one that swerves from the traditional emphasis on "family, neighborhood, church, lodge, and school to race, gender, occupation, and sexual preference."

These ideological divisions within U.S. society threaten to rend the nation into hostile factions. For example, Richard Bernstein, in *Dictatorship of Virtue: Multiculturalism and the Battle for America's Future*, brands ideological multiculturalists as "radical-left inhabitants of a political dreamland." Its critics maintain that multiculturalism is not—and never can be—a viable educational principle.

Thomas J. Famularo, *USA Today Magazine*, May 1996.

Identity politics, radical feminism, multiculturalism, and educating for difference all march these days under the innocent-sounding umbrella of Diversity. It is out of respect for Diversity that universities commit themselves to racial and gender quotas and preferences in hiring (New Hampshire's "eighteen by 2005"); racial and ethnic quotas and preferences in student admissions (New Hampshire's "fourfold increase"); mandatory sensitivity training (New Hampshire's "prejudice-reduction workshop," Springfield College's faculty circle-walk, West Virginia's "educational remediation"); the creation of women's studies programs, African-American studies programs, ethnic studies programs, and lesbian-gay-bisexual-gender studies programs, even when devoid of intellectual content (New Paltz's "Revolting Behavior" workshops); and, of course, the ubiquitous speech codes (Penn and WVU).

The resources universities devote to sustaining an atmosphere friendly to these post-1965 innovations are truly remarkable. On nearly every campus, a bureaucracy of residence life advisers, multicultural affairs offices, women's centers (for feminists only), ethnic dormitories and social centers, and special services for gay, lesbian, and transgendered students now exists. The perpetuation of this bureaucracy depends on its ability to satisfy any and all demands made on the basis of group identity, as defined by race, ethnicity, gender, and sexual orientation. And as students come to realize early on that their racial, sexual, and ethnic attributes are the aspects of themselves most cherished by the university, so they learn to make their demands on the basis of those attributes. The result is a spiral of ever more strident and impossible demands by an ever-increasing number of ethnic and sexual groups addressed to university employees whose professional *raison d'être* is to foster group-based identities in the name of Diversity. Of course, there are exceptions: taking pride in and making demands on the basis of one's European descent, maleness, or heterosexuality will fail to attract the university's patronage; indeed, such behavior could very well lead to disciplinary proceedings for its racism, sexism, and homophobia.

Multicultural Tension

That identity politics has a peculiar hold on the minds of today's students can be seen by looking at the recently published book *When Hope and Fear Collide: A Portrait of Today's College Student*. Written by the president of Teachers College at Columbia University, Arthur Levine, and his research assistant, Jeanette Cureton, the book is based on extensive surveys, interviews, and site visits with students and administrators on American campuses of every variety. In its chapter on multiculturalism, one reads of what the authors call "multicultural tension" on the campuses fueled by the following student characteristics: a "preoccupation with differences," the "mitosis of student groups," "segregation of students" by race and ethnicity, and a "growing sense of victimization." Whereas students they interviewed in the late 1970s described themselves in terms of what they had in common with their generation, current students were remarkably different. When faced with the same questions as their predecessors, they emphasized the characteristics that made them unique or different: race, gender, geography, sexual orientation, ethnicity, and religion. For example, one student said he grew up in a small town in which he was one of a handful of Asian Americans in his school. He said he never thought of his Asian roots as being important until he got to college. By the end of his freshman year, he realized it was the most important aspect of his being.

One does not have to think that the ethnic roots of one's family tree are trivial to be deeply troubled by this portrait. How could it be that a student who thought little of his racial and ethnic roots before arriving at his university had, by the end of his freshman year, become convinced that those characteristics defined his essence as a human being? I have already provided the answer. It is unlikely that this student's new understanding of what it means to be a human being was arrived at through serious intellectual inquiry. Since the 1960s, there has been a near total collapse of general-education requirements that lead students to a sustained and rigorous confrontation with the greatest minds and the most thorough scholarship on the human condition—to say nothing of the decline of foreign language study, the window into truly foreign cultures. (See the National Association of Scholars' report, *The Dissolution of General Education: 1914–1993*.) One can also reasonably doubt that this student had ever set foot in Asia, that he had ever studied an Asian language, or that he had ever read a serious book on an Asian culture.

A Distortion of Diversity

It would be a mistake to excuse the university's agency in promoting diversity, thus understood, as simply an accommodation to the multi-ethnic, sexually heterodox nature of today's student body. The consequences for the intellectual life of the university are serious, so serious as to warrant our viewing the aggressive promotion of the multicultural agenda as an assault on the academic enterprise.

The dogmatic and partisan nature of the academy's current interest in diversity is easy to demonstrate. As Kors and Silverglate observe in *The Shadow University*, all the talk about celebrating diversity excludes from the celebration, or far better than celebration, the study and deeper under-standing of "evangelical, fundamentalist, Protestant cul-ture," or "traditionalist Catholic culture," or the "gender roles of Orthodox Jewish or of Shiite Islamic culture," or of "black American Pentecostal culture," or of assimilation, or of the "white, rural South," to say nothing of cultures that require mastery of non-English languages and training in historical method for genuine understanding. Instead, the categories of culture that are recognized by the orthodox academic notion of diversity and multiculturalism are aston-ishingly limited—race and ethnicity (but only race and eth-nicity that has experienced oppression), gender (but only as defined by academic feminism), and sexual orientation (with only gay, lesbian, and transgendered identities being worthy of celebration and sympathetic study; heterosexuality is the mark of the oppressor). That this constitutes a terrible dis-tortion of the real diversity found in human nature and cul-ture is apparent. Just as obvious is its potential to channel the wellsprings of human thought and action into a dangerous provincialism, denying both the reality and the legitimacy of the individual and the universal, affirming only the approved group.

Politicizing Academic Life

Up to this point, my primary focus has been on what Kors and Silverglate dub the shadow university, university life be-yond the classroom. The politicization of academic life has respected no such boundaries, however. Indeed, it began in the 1960s with an attack on the classroom. Back then, the demand of radical students was that the classroom be made *relevant*, meaning relevant to their desire to escape from and to put an end to a war which they opposed and a culture they believed somehow made that war inevitable. The objectivity of scholars, with its appearance of indifference to or critical distance from the task at hand, was quickly rendered con-temptible as nothing more than an obstacle to determined action. Indeed, the objective scholar, far from being re-spected as an independent observer or critic of democratic enthusiasms, was seen as an accomplice in the crimes of the American regime. The demand for political relevance has now morphed into identity politics and the demand for sensitivity to the claims and self-esteem of an ever-expanding list of groups defined by racial, ethnic, and sexual common denominators. The old relevance and the new sensitivity are both the result of the rejection of, and hostility to, the model of disinterested, objective scholarship, with its refusal to take its bearings from the immediate, often transitory, passions and interests of the society beyond the university's gates. . . .

Curriculum studies by both the National Association of Scholars and the Association of American Colleges and Universities (the latter a promoter of Diversity) have found diversity requirements in a substantial majority of today's colleges, where no such requirements existed in the 1960s. It is certainly true that some of the courses that meet those core requirements follow the model of the study of non-Western cultures found in traditional liberal arts curricula. But most of the courses meeting the diversity requirements do not focus on the study of foreign cultures, but rather on the study of Americans, such as the "Recognition and Affirmation of Difference Requirement" at Carleton College, and the many courses with titles such as "Classism, Racism, and Sexism," "Race and Gender in U.S. Society," and "Introduction to Lesbian and Gay Studies." These courses, with few exceptions, are politicized "oppression studies," as one learns by visiting the websites of the National Women's Studies Association and the Gay and Lesbian Studies Association. In the meantime, only one out of the top fifty universities in the country required undergraduates to take an introductory history course, such as Western Civilization, in 1993, down from 60 percent of the same universities in 1964. . . .

Compromising Academic Integrity

American institutions of higher learning have deeply compromised their claims to academic integrity in their rush to embrace what they regard as politically progressive reforms in the name of Diversity. Intellectual and aesthetic standards—sought after, argued over and used to guide qualitative judgment since the dawn of reason—have been jettisoned to the point where appeals to the blatantly political principle of racial, ethnic, and sexual representation are permitted to determine the choice of works to be studied and courses to be offered.

The culture wars in higher education are not between a political left and a political right, or between liberals and conservatives. They are between those who wish to politicize academic life as part of a larger agenda of social transformation, and those who see in the university the only institution in American life where knowledge is valued for its own sake, where students can be forgiven a temporary lack of social concern and engagement for the sake of remedying a more fundamental deprivation, their lack of self-knowledge. The cure, insofar as there is one, is to be found in a liberal education, not in an identity-fix offered by the latest multicultural initiative.

Whether the institutional life of higher education any longer has room for liberal education is an open question. Our students have lost the art of reading; our colleges no longer encourage them to read and love beautiful and profound texts; and our administrators and most of our current faculties themselves have little experience with the kind of education those texts represent and the kind of truth they seek. If we care about the highest in human nature, however, we have no more urgent task than to attempt, perhaps against the odds, the restoration of liberal learning.

Periodical Bibliography

The following articles have been selected to supplement the diverse views presented in this chapter.

Richard Cimino — "Back Toward Orthodoxy: A Conservative Resurgence Sweeps American Religion," *American Enterprise*, April/May 2002.

Randy Cohen — "The Politics of Ethics: By Identifying Ethics with Civic Virtue, We Create an Ethics of the Left," *The Nation*, April 8, 2002.

Dinesh D'Souza — "What's So Great About America?" *American Enterprise*, April/May 2002.

Barbara Ehrenreich — "Everything I Like About Religion I Learned from an Atheist," *The Humanist*, November 1999.

Edward D. Ericson Jr. — "America's Religious Disconnect," *American Outlook*, November/December 2000.

Tom Garrison — "Why I Left the Left," *Liberty*, January 2000.

Gary Glenn and John Stack — "America: Fundamentally Religious," *World & I*, December 1999.

William B. Irvine — "Confronting Relativism," *Academic Questions*, Winter 2000.

John Leo — "Accidental Conspirator," *U.S. News & World Report*, June 12, 2000.

John O'Sullivan — "Types of Right: How the Conservatives Break Down," *National Review*, October 11, 1999.

Laura Saponara — "Confronting the Logic of the New Right," *Peace Review*, Winter 1999.

Arthur M. Schlesinger Jr. — "A Question of Power," *American Prospect*, April 23, 2001.

Daniel Taylor — "Deconstructing the Gospel of Tolerance," *Christianity Today*, January 11, 1999.

Jason Toon — "What's a Progressive to Do?" *Progressive Populist*, November 15, 2001.

Robert Wuthnow — "The Moral Minority," *American Prospect*, May 22, 2000.

CHAPTER 4

Should Government Regulate Cultural Values?

Chapter Preface

One of the most long-standing culture wars debates is the question of what role the government should play in fostering moral behavior in individuals and communities. Although the government often intervenes in matters of morality—when, for example, it passes laws that prohibit obviously harmful behaviors—disagreement abounds when issues such as divorce, teen pregnancy, abortion, or homosexuality are targeted for government regulation.

In 1998, for example, a board established by the Chicago Divinity School and the Institute for American Values released a report entitled *A Call to Civil Society: Why Democracy Needs Moral Truths.* Prompted by concerns over America's declining moral standards, the board's goals were to "rediscover the existence of transmittable moral truth" and offer proposals to strengthen the traditional family and promote "cultural and moral renewal." The report recommended enacting laws that would make divorce more difficult to obtain and establishing government-funded housing policies that granted preference to two-parent families. The board also suggested allowing school districts to ban pregnant students from classrooms in order to "send the message that teenage pregnancy is undesirable and should not be condoned."

Liberals broadly condemned the report, charging that it was an attempt on the part of social conservatives to impose their idea of morality on society. Many question whether America was really better off in the days when divorce was difficult to obtain and when pregnant teens were forced to drop out of school. In a country with such a diverse population, such efforts to "legislate morality" are untenable and undemocratic, liberals contend. As syndicated columnist Cynthia Tucker maintains, advocates of so-called moral renewal would invade privacy and curb individual freedom: "The ultraconservatives want control of the country. They want to tell the rest of us how to live, where to pray, what to think, how to love." Rather than enacting laws that would discriminate against alleged "moral offenders," liberals argue, the government should seek ways to promote tolerance. The passage of civil rights laws in the 1960s, which made racial discrimination illegal, is one example of a federal regulation that fosters tolerance, liberals point out. On the other hand, many conservatives maintain that the success of civil rights laws actually proves that government can and should seek to change society's moral standards.

In the following chapter, authors representing different points on the political spectrum elaborate further on governmental regulation of morality and cultural values.

"Can governments legislate moral issues?
Of course."

The Government Should Legislate Morality

Gregory Maturi

In the following viewpoint, Gregory Maturi argues that governments can and should legislate morality. Those who believe that morality should not be legislated often claim that doing so involves governmental imposition of religious beliefs on society. However, Maturi explains, public morality is actually defined by commonly shared principles about acceptable public behavior, not by any particular religion. While it may be difficult to establish public consensus on controversial issues such as abortion or suicide, reasoned argument on these issues can help guide and construct law. Thus, the government provides a means through which people of differing opinions debate and legislate morality. Maturi, a Catholic priest, is the associate director of the Catholic Center at New York University.

As you read, consider the following questions:
1. What is the difference between religion and public morality, according to Maturi?
2. According to the author, what did Prohibition reveal about governmental legislation of morality?
3. In Maturi's opinion, what skills are required of religious believers who wish to shape law?

M any wonder what law and morality have to do with each other. Some assume that if we're talking about morality then we must be talking about religion, and religion has nothing to do with law. But morality and religion are not the same thing. While most Americans feel uncomfortable mixing law and religion, many are greatly concerned about issues of public morality. They understand, at least instinctively, that there is a difference between religion (faith and an institutional church) and public morality (questions that affect the public square and what behavior is acceptable in public). Law is concerned with public behavior and as such is concerned with moral issues. This brief essay examines how moral issues shape public law.

Morality and Law

Some claim that you can't legislate morality. But is that true? If by legislating morality they mean taking something that is immoral and making it a crime, we do that all the time. Take, for example, theft. Theft is a moral issue that has been put into law. It is both immoral and illegal. Another example, though one not often thought of as a moral issue, is smoking. Laws that restrict smoking are moral in nature. Why? Any time the law says "do this" or "don't do that" it is evaluating whether an action is good or bad. That's a moral judgment. There are a series of laws that restrict smoking because some have decided that it is not good to smoke. It may be objected that smoking is a health issue and not a moral issue. But is there really a difference between a public health issue and a public moral issue? Take, for example, the issue of abortion. Abortion is often put forth as a health issue, but the minute the law tries to restrict it, the same people quickly perceive it as a moral issue and say "don't impose your morality." I agree that abortion is a moral issue. Most issues of law are.

Not all attempts to legislate morality have been successful. Prohibition, for example, was an attempt in this country to outlaw liquor. It was a moral issue, strongly religiously motivated, that was put into law. Unfortunately Prohibition turned out to be a terrible failure and the laws were eventually repealed. Far from proving that you can't legislate morality, however, Prohibition proved that the federal government should not try to legislate moral issues traditionally left at the local level. Currently Prohibition laws remain at the local level in some states, and to a large extent they work. Can governments legislate moral issues? Of course. Will it be effective? In some cases yes, in other cases no. It requires prudential judgment and reasoned moral principles on the part of elected officials to decide when and how to legislate morality. My only point is that moral issues can legitimately shape law.

Moreover, morality should shape law. Take, for example, the issue of racial desegregation. To a large extent the motivations and arguments for integration were moral and religious. Despite the fact that there was no clear consensus among the American people, desegregation went into law, and although it has taken a long time, we have seen a change of attitude brought about by taking a moral position and putting it into law.

Reason as a Common Ground

Unfortunately moral issues are sometimes construed as religious issues, especially when they are put forth by religious people. In such a case the issues are perceived as imposing religious beliefs. But is that the case? Many of the views religious people hold are not a matter of faith, but depend rather on reason. Reason is not exclusive to any religion, but is part of the make-up of the human person. Everyone has the ability to reason independent of one's religious beliefs. Morality has reason as a common ground that can be shared by all people, even by those who don't believe in God but who strive to use their intelligence to find answers to common problems.

Perhaps part of the problem is that religious people don't always distinguish what they know by faith from what they know by reason. Faith and reason act in their life like a stereo which has both a faith channel and a reason channel and in practice both channels blend together. Consequently, those who are not religious look at what is said and done by believers and conclude that it is said or done out of faith. While that may be the case in many instances, it doesn't mean that their position can't be explained or defended in terms of reason. People who don't share a common religion can still discuss moral issues in terms of the common ground of reason. Morality is simply reason applied to human behavior.

The Law Can Encourage Morality

Some liberals complain that opponents of abortion are "just trying to legislate morality." There are libertarians who say the same thing about people who want to regulate pornography and drug use. Some conservatives reject all attempts to legislate matters of economic behavior on the same basis. Across the political spectrum, lots of people seem to agree: You cannot legislate morality.

Why not? The law cannot force people to make good choices. It can, however, encourage people to develop new ways of thinking, seeing and feeling. Habits and practices we initially adopt to conform to authority can start to make sense to us over time. Sometimes it may take the pressure of an external demand to force us to see the value in a choice or a way of life we might otherwise dismiss. So, even though the law cannot compel us to make good choices, it can help us, at least indirectly, to change and grow morally. Someone who says it is impossible to legislate morality may be technically correct, but the law can certainly make a morally important difference in people's lives.

David Pendleton, *America*, February 21, 1998.

Historically, individual states had established churches, though never at the federal level. Thus, it was expected that religion should be included in public debate about law. Still, it was expected that when one entered into public debate, the debate was carried out not in religious terms, but in terms that all could relate to, even if the motivation for entering the debate was religious in nature. Because we live in a pluralistic society, when we argue we argue in terms of reason. That does not mean we banish all reference to religion. Rather, it means that religious believers who wish to shape law must be able to explain to others who do not share their religious beliefs why their ideas are based on fundamental principles of morality commonly shared and not peculiar to any particular religious belief.

Still, there remains a hesitancy to listen to what is said

with religious conviction. When a religious person enters the public debate, even if he or she does so solely with arguments of reason, it is still perceived as "the church" interfering with politics. Again, this is mere prejudice. Take, for example, the issue of stealing. Would anyone object to a church speaking out against stealing? Probably not. But isn't stealing a sin? Yet, one doesn't have to be a believer to know that stealing is wrong. Theft is wrong not because a particular religion says it is, but because reason tells us it is, and therefore it is incorporated into law. When the church encourages a law against stealing it is not interfering in politics. Religion can support the things reason can come to know.

Establishing Consensus

Of course, theft is not a problem because it is not controversial. But what about controversial issues such as abortion or suicide? How can morality shape the law on such issues? In the beginning of this country there was a lot of consensus on moral issues. Changes in population created religious and ethnic diversity that have led to a breakdown in consensus. In order for morality to shape public law effectively, there needs to be a consensus. But how do we establish consensus? It requires debate, authentic discussion, and a closer scrutiny of the arguments behind the issues. When consensus breaks down on a particular moral issue one has to ask whether reasonable arguments exist for a particular position. For example, is it reasonable to prohibit suicide? In order to build consensus the weight of the discussion needs to fall upon the reasoning of the arguments. Rather than recoil from moral issues, Americans need the intellectual courage and vitality to reason through them.

Militating against such intellectual integrity is the ever present temptation to personal attacks. We live in an age greatly influenced by Freudian psychology. When someone makes an argument there is the tendency not to listen to the merits of the argument but to psychoanalyze the person making the argument. Instead of examining the argument itself, people ask questions like, "Why are they making this argument?" or "What is their interest in this issue?" But it's important to distinguish motivation, the reason why someone says or does something, from the reasons for their position themselves. For example, when religious people make arguments against abortion from a reasoned point of view, it is still claimed to be a religious issue. We need to distinguish motivation from the actual argument if there is to be any hope of a civil public debate on disputed issues. In the past such problems were avoided by using pseudonyms to disguise the person making the argument. Since the person's background was unknown and could not be considered, opponents were forced to face the argument itself. That made for better public debate.

In conclusion, moral issues inevitably shape public law. Justice demands that law be stable and consistent. To this end we need authentic debate that examines the reasons underlying moral issues. Only in this way can morality rightly shape public law.

| "What fools we are when we think we can legislate away human immorality."

The Government Cannot Legislate Morality

Charles Colson

In the following viewpoint, which was written in the wake of several major corporate scandals during 2001 and 2002, Charles Colson maintains that it is impossible for government to legislate morality. He contends that although laws and government regulations are necessary, they ultimately cannot force people to be ethical, nor can they solve society's enduring problems. The nation will avert scandals and moral decline only when Americans embrace a common set of values that fosters the desire to do what is right, the author concludes. Colson is chairman of Prison Fellowship Ministries, a volunteer Christian group that provides outreach to prisoners, ex-prisoners, crime victims, and their families.

As you read, consider the following questions:
1. What major political scandal was the author of this viewpoint involved in?
2. What ineffective governmental reforms were passed as a result of the Watergate scandal, according to Colson?
3. What is the real hope for corporate America, in the author's opinion?

Charles Colson, "Law Isn't Enough," *Washington Post*, July 30, 2002, p. A17. Copyright © 2002 by Washington Post Writers Group. Reproduced by permission of the author.

President George W. Bush said recently [in response to the corporate scandals of 2001 and 2002], "There is no capitalism without conscience; there is no wealth without character." Many, including the *Washington Post*, responded that conscience has nothing to do with it. "There's no harm in this rhetoric," said the *Post*, "but it is naive to suppose that business can be regulated by some kind of national honor code."

Will we never learn? When I was in the White House serving President Richard Nixon, I knew what the law was. I was trained in it. There were plenty of laws on the books forbidding precisely the kind of abuses into which we rationalized ourselves. If I had ever sat down and thought about it, I would have realized that we were backing into a serious conspiracy that could topple a president. By the time I did realize it and warned the president, it was too late.

Are Laws a Deterrent?

Watergate did not happen for want of laws. It happened because people cut corners, did what they thought was necessary for the president to survive and covered up their own misdeeds while rationalizing it all as being in the interest of the country. Is anyone so naive as to think laws could have changed this?

The laws existing at that time could have sent any of us away for 10 years or more. Was that not a deterrent? In the wake of Watergate came the same hue and cry we hear in Congress and in the press today: Toughen up; crack down; send people to jail. So we enacted an array of new campaign finance laws, reformed the intelligence apparatus so a president could not misuse it and toughened up criminal statutes.

Did we usher in a period of good government—no more scandals? Hardly. We had Iran-Contra,[1] followed by the Clinton scandals[2] that resulted in impeachment. And this Con-

---

1. A reference to the 1983–1988 scandal in which some Reagan administration officials funneled money from illegal arms sales in Iran to the Contras, a counterrevolutionary group attempting to overthrow the government of Nicaragua.   2. In the "Whitewater scandal" during his 1992–2000 presidency, Bill Clinton was accused of having illegally used his political influence when he was governor of Arkansas in 1978. Specifically, critics claimed that he assisted in a land development deal in return for campaign contributions. In 1998, Clinton admitted that he had a relationship of a sexual nature with White House intern Monica Lewinsky.

gress has now thrown out all the Watergate-era reforms because they failed to work. As Samuel Johnson put it, "How small of all that human hearts endure/That part which kings or laws can cause or cure."

The Need to Cultivate Conscience

What fools we are when we think we can legislate away human immorality. We certainly need laws, but I stand as living proof that the cure comes not from laws and statutes but from the transforming of the human heart—the embracing of a moral code to which conscience is bound. The real hope for corporate America lies in cultivating conscience, a disposition to know and do what is right. And yet I have surveyed business school curricula and find that hardly any teach ethics.

Any society that hopes to survive as a free society has to have a moral code that the vast majority of citizens embrace. It is naive to say that everyone is able to do whatever is right in his or her own eyes and then be astonished by the moral chaos that follows. The death of a common morality threatens our very liberty, because without individual conscience, society cannot be held in check except through coercion.

The Government Cannot Teach Morality

Teaching morality is the province of parents and religion. If they fail, the government can't do it instead. George Washington's argument is still valid. He said republican government depends on a virtuous people. No means of instilling virtue has been found to be superior to religion. Therefore, he said, anyone who is an enemy of religion is an enemy of republican government.

A government cannot make bad people good, but good people can make bad government good.

Charley Reese, *Conservative Chronicle*, August 19, 1998.

But even coercion ultimately fails. There is no police force large enough to keep an eye on every individual. "This country ought to have, when it is healthy and when it is working as it is intended to work, 250 million policemen—called conscience," says Michael Novak. "When there are 250 million consciences on guard, it's surprising how few police are needed on the streets."

If we believe that our greatest need is new laws and regulations, we miss the great lesson of this scandal—and all the scandals that have gone before it. We will pass a whole series of laws, many of which, as Watergate demonstrates, will later be repealed when the next round of scandals proves them ineffective. The alternative is to take a bracing dose of reality, to recognize that the enemy is moral relativism and confusion, to embrace once again a solid code by which morality can be informed and then to go about the business of strengthening the conscience of the nation.

Our most intractable social problems cannot be solved by public policy but only by the practice of moral behavior. The president is not naive; he is dead right—without conscience, capitalism fails.

> *"Separation of religion and government is essential to religious liberty, freedom of conscience, and democratic values."*

The Government Must Maintain the Separation of Church and State

Edd Doerr

Edd Doerr is president of the American Humanist Association and Americans for Religious Liberty. In the following viewpoint, Doerr argues that the separation of government and religion is essential to a free and democratic society. The government should not favor any one religion; nor should it provide nonpreferential aid to all religions. If the wall of separation between church and state were to break down, Doerr contends, sectarian interests could use the government to impose their beliefs on the population.

As you read, consider the following questions:
1. According to Doerr, when and by whom was the phrase "a wall of separation between Church and State" first coined?
2. According to Supreme Court Justice Hugo Black, quoted by the author, what is the intention of the "establishment of religion" clause of the First Amendment?
3. What specific things could happen if the wall of church-state separation crumbles, in Doerr's opinion?

Edd Doerr, "Jefferson's Wall . . . ," *The Humanist*, vol. 62, January/February 2002, pp. 10–12. Copyright © 2002 by the American Humanist Association. Reproduced by permission of the author.

Two hundred years ago, on January 1, 1802, President Thomas Jefferson penned a letter destined to be ranked with the Declaration of Independence, James Madison's 1785 Memorial and Remonstrance Against Religious Assessments, the U.S. Constitution, the Bill of Rights, and George Washington's 1790 letter to the Touro Synagogue in Newport, Rhode Island.

Addressed to the Danbury, Connecticut, Baptist Association, Jefferson's letter stated, in part:

> Believing with you that religion is a matter which lies solely between man and his God, that he owes account to none other for his faith or his worship, that the legislative powers of government reach actions only, and not opinions, I contemplate with sovereign reverence that act of the whole American people [the First Amendment] which declared that their legislature should "make no law respecting an establishment of religion, or prohibiting the free exercise thereof," thus building a wall of separation between Church and State.

The importance of this letter can only be grasped in its historical context. . . .

An Influential Metaphor

Jefferson's "wall of separation" metaphor was employed by the Supreme Court in 1879 in its first religious liberty case, *Reynolds v. United States*. Citing the Jefferson quote above, the Court held that "coming as this does from an acknowledged leader of the advocates of the measure, it may be accepted almost as an authoritative declaration of the scope and effect of the amendment thus secured."

The next time the High Court utilized "the wall" was in the landmark 1947 case, *Everson v. Board of Education*. The Court stated, in Justice Hugo Black's ringing words:

> The "establishment of religion" clause of the First Amendment means at least this: Neither a state nor the Federal Government can set up a church. Neither can pass laws which aid one religion, aid all religions, or prefer one religion over another. Neither can force nor influence a person to go to or remain away from church against his will or force him to profess a belief or disbelief in any religion. No person can be punished for entertaining or professing religious beliefs or disbeliefs, for church attendance or nonattendance.

No tax in any amount, large or small, can be levied to support any religious activities or institutions, whatever they may be called, or whatever form they may adopt to teach or practice religion. Neither a state nor the Federal Government can, openly or secretly, participate in the affairs of any religious organizations or groups and vice versa. In the words of Jefferson, the clause against establishment of religion by law was intended to erect "a wall of separation between church and state.". . . That wall must be kept high and impregnable.

The *Everson* passage was approved by every member of the 1947 Court, was cited favorably in three subsequent rulings, and its spirit has informed many more. However, thanks to several conservative appointments, the Supreme Court has been drifting slowly away from the position of the *Everson* justices and such subsequent "separationists" as the late, highly regarded Justices William J. Brennan, Thurgood Marshall, and Harry Blackmun and toward the "accommodationist" stance of Justices William Rehnquist, Antonin Scalia, and Clarence Thomas. The latter have made it quite clear that they don't agree with Jefferson, the *Everson* Court, and the earlier Court majorities. Before the end of the present Court's current term in July 2002, we will find out whether the serving justices will uphold Jefferson's wall or consign it to the rubbish heap. The crucial test will be a case involving a thus far successful challenge to an Ohio law that provides subsidies through vouchers to sectarian schools in Cleveland—a case scheduled for hearing within weeks. [The Supreme Court ruled in favor of school vouchers.]

Trouble for Religious Freedom

It cannot be denied that if Jefferson's wall is allowed to crumble, religious freedom in the United States will be in serious trouble. The door will be open for sectarian religion to invade public education; for women to be chained to medieval sectarian medical codes; and for government to compel taxpayers to support sectarian schools and other institutions that commonly practice forms of discrimination and indoctrination the vast majority of Americans would find intolerable.

To understand our present predicament we must return to Jefferson's 1802 letter to the Danbury Baptists, which latter-day "accommodationists"—heirs of Virginia Governor Patrick Henry, who was defeated by Jefferson and James Madison in 1785–1786—will do anything to discredit. Typical of accommodationist attacks is the one made twenty years ago at a Senate hearing on then-President Ronald Reagan's school prayer amendment by televangelist Pat Robertson—the same Pat Robertson who joined with Jerry Falwell shortly after the terrorist attacks on September 11, 2001, in suggesting that God allowed the tragedy to take place to punish Americans for their "liberal sins." Robertson has misrepresented the Jefferson letter and said that the "wall" metaphor "only appeared in the constitution of the Communist Soviet Union." (Details may be found in Robert S. Alley's 1996 book, *Public Education and the Public Good.*)

Auth. © 2000 by *The Philadelphia Inquirer.* Reprinted by permission of Universal Press Syndicate.

In reality, Jefferson's letter was a response to a letter from the Danbury Baptists praising him and voicing a complaint against Connecticut's establishment of the Congregational Church, an arrangement finally ended in 1818. Jefferson received the letter on December 30 and replied two days later. Although Chief Justice Rehnquist brushed off Jefferson's letter in a 1985 ruling as merely "a short note of courtesy," our third president took it a great deal more seriously.

Jefferson sent the Baptists' original letter along with a draft of his reply to Attorney General Levi Lincoln with this request:

> The Baptist address, now enclosed, admits of a condemnation of the alliance between Church and State, under the authority of the Constitution. It furnishes an occasion, too, which I have long wished to find, of saying why I do not proclaim fastings and thanksgivings, as my predecessor did. The address, to be sure, does not point at this, and its introduction is awkward. But I foresee no opportunity of doing it more pertinently. I know it will give great offense to the New England clergy; but the advocate of religious freedom is to expect neither peace nor forgiveness from them. Will you be so good as to examine the answer and suggest any alterations which might prevent an ill effect, or promote a good one, among the people?

At Lincoln's suggestion, Jefferson omitted his comments about proclamations so as not to "give uneasiness to some of our republican friends in the eastern states where the proclamation of thanksgivings etc. by their Executive is an antient [sic] habit and is respected."

The Importance of Church-State Separation

Another attack by accommodationists on Jefferson's "wall" is their insistence that the First Amendment's establishment clause was intended not to erect a wall but to permit nonpreferential aid to all religions. That, of course, was the Patrick Henry position, which Madison and Jefferson defeated in the Virginia legislature the year before the Constitutional Convention was held in Philadelphia. The nonpreferentialist, accommodationist position was considered by the First Congress in 1789 and rejected in favor of the present language of the First Amendment.

Nor was the establishment clause drafted simply to block a single religious "establishment," as some accommodationists claim. By 1789 the colonial, European-style single establishments were virtually a dead letter, having given way to church-state separation, as in Virginia, or some sort of broad multiple establishment.

No establishment of religion means what Jefferson and

Madison intended, what Washington lauded in his 1790 letter to the Touro Synagogue, what the Supreme Court held in 1947 and for decades afterward, and what far-sighted religious leaders, politicians, and ordinary people have always believed. The American experience has proven that separation of church and state is best for religion, for democratic government, and for the liberties of the people. The alternative is some greater or lesser form of Talibanization,* the goofy agendas of Falwell and Robertson, or the dismal, disastrous dystopia sought by the sectarian special interests seeking school vouchers, tax support for faith-based initiatives, organized school prayer, and the imposition on women of narrow theologies of embryonic personhood.

If history teaches anything, it is that separation of religion and government is essential to religious liberty, freedom of conscience, and democratic values.

---

* A reference to the Taliban, an Islamic fundamentalist sect that ruled Afghanistan from 1996–2001. The Taliban became notorious for its suppression of women and strict limitations on freedom of expression.

*"The wall of separation between church
and state is a metaphor based upon bad
history. . . . It should be frankly and
explicitly abandoned."*

The Separation of Church and State Harms American Culture

Roy S. Moore

The doctrine of the separation of church and state has been misinterpreted in a way that limits religious freedom, contends Roy S. Moore in the following viewpoint. Because church-state separation is often taken to mean that government cannot support religion in any way, Christians and Jews are denied their right to express their beliefs while participating in public forums or state-funded activities. However, Moore explains, the ideal of church-state separation was actually intended to keep the government from prescribing what one's faith should be—not to preclude people from publicly acknowledging God. The government's banning of religious activity and prayer in public schools and other public venues has contributed to America's moral decline, the author concludes. Moore is a circuit judge for the sixteenth judicial district in Etowah County, Alabama.

As you read, consider the following questions:
1. According to Moore, what are some specific examples that reveal the government's bias against public worship?
2. How did John Locke define the church-state relationship, according to the author?
3. In Moore's view, what historical precedents reveal the true relationship between religion and government?

Roy S. Moore, "Putting God Back in the Public Square," *USA Today Magazine*, vol. 129, September 2000, p. 51. Copyright © 2000 by the Society for the Advancement of Education. Reproduced by permission.

In his first official act, Pres. George Washington did something that would be unthinkable today: He prayed in public! Specifically, during his inaugural address, he made "fervent supplications to that Almighty Being who rules over the universe, who presides in the councils of nations, and whose providential aids can supply every human defect, that His benediction may consecrate to the liberties and happiness of the people of the United States a Government instituted by themselves for these essential purposes. . . . No people can be bound to acknowledge and adore the Invisible Hand which conducts the affairs of men more than the people of the United States. Every step by which they have advanced to the character of an independent nation seems to have been distinguished by some token of providential agency."

If that were not enough, Washington added: "We ought to be no less persuaded that the propitious smiles of Heaven can never be expected on a nation that disregards the eternal rules of order and right which Heaven itself has ordained."

More than 200 years later, few government officials are bold enough to make earnest professions of faith. It seems that politicians can do just about anything in public but pray, unless it is obligatory (say, during an annual prayer breakfast at the White House). They can survive scandal and immoral conduct, but they suffer ostracism and worse once they are labeled members of the "Religious Right."

A Bias Against Public Worship

Even the American justice system, which is firmly rooted in the Judeo-Christian tradition, has developed a bias against public worship and the public acknowledgment of God that ought to give the most militant atheist cause for concern. If judges can deny Christians and Jews the right to express their beliefs in the public square, they can surely deny secular humanists (devout believers of a different sort) the same right.

• In California, creches and crosses have been removed from downtown Christmas and Easter displays.

• In Kansas, city hall monuments featuring religious symbols have been torn down.

• In Rhode Island, high school graduation invocations and benedictions have been banned.

• In Alabama, students have been prohibited by Federal court order from praying, distributing religious materials, and even discussing anything of a devotional or inspirational nature with their classmates and teachers.

• In Ohio, an appellate court has overturned the sentence of a man convicted of raping an eight-year-old child 10 times. Why? Because the judge who pronounced the sentence quoted from the 18th chapter of Matthew: "But whoso shall offend one of these little ones which believe in me, it were better for him that a millstone were hanged about his neck, and that he were drowned in the depth of the sea."

In the courtroom in which I preside, the public display of the Ten Commandments and voluntary clergy-led prayer prior to jury organizational sessions have sparked not only a national controversy, but an epic legal battle. In 1995, I was sued in Federal court by the American Civil Liberties Union (ACLU) and the Alabama Freethought Association. Just prior to that case being dismissed for lack of standing (the ACLU and Alabama Freethought Association failed to show that they had been or were about to be injured), a separate lawsuit was filed in Alabama state court requesting a ruling on whether the First Amendment to the Constitution prohibits the display of the Ten Commandments and voluntary prayer in the courtroom. A state circuit court judge presiding in Montgomery County, Ala., held that the practices in Etowah County were unconstitutional under the First Amendment's "Establishment Clause," which reads, "Congress shall make no law respecting an establishment of religion. . . ."It would appear that the circuit court judge and others were not impressed when the members of the House of Representatives and the Senate passed a resolution stating that: "the Ten Commandments are a declaration of fundamental principles that are the cornerstones of a fair and just society; and the public display, including display in government offices and courthouses, of the Ten Commandments should be permitted."

The state circuit court's ruling was appealed to the Alabama Supreme Court, which set it aside in 1998. Nevertheless, Federal constitutional issues regarding public worship and the public acknowledgment of God remain unresolved.

The "Wall of Separation"

In a 1997 law review article, Brian T. Collidge expressed the opinion of many in the legal profession when he claimed that the mere display of the Ten Commandments in the courtroom is a "dangerous" practice. Although Collidge concedes that the Commandments reflect universal teachings that are beneficial to a civil society, they make explicit references to God, and, in his view, this is an unconstitutional breach of the "wall of separation between church and state."

This now-famous "wall of separation" phrase does not appear in the Constitution, Declaration of Independence, Articles of Confederation, or any other official American document, yet millions of Americans have been led to believe that it does and that, in the words found in a 1947 Supreme Court decision, "The wall must be kept high and impregnable."

The phrase is actually mentioned for the first time in a letter Pres. Thomas Jefferson wrote in 1802 in reply to an inquiry from the Danbury Baptist Association: "Believing with you that religion is a matter which lies solely between man and his God, that he owes account to none other for his faith or his worship; that the legislative powers of the government reach actions only, and not opinions, I contemplate with sovereign reverence that act of the whole American people which declared that their legislature should make no law respecting an establishment of religion, or prohibiting the free exercise thereof, thus building a wall of separation between church and state."

Yet, did Jefferson mean that the government should in no way support religion? To find the answer, we must go back more than 100 years before he wrote to the Danbury Baptist Association. Jefferson was strongly influenced by John Locke, a well-known English philosopher, who published "A Letter Concerning Toleration" in 1689 wherein he clearly defined the proper church-state relationship. Locke stated that "The magistrate has no power to enforce by law, either in his own Church, or much less in another, the use of any rites or forms of worship by the force of his laws."

Herein lies the true meaning of separation between church and state as the concept was understood by Jefferson and the other Founding Fathers: Government may never dictate one's form of worship or articles of faith. Not all public worship of God must be halted; on the contrary, freedom to engage in such worship was the very reason for creating a doctrine of separation between church and state.

Two days after he wrote to the Danbury Baptist Association, Jefferson attended a church service conducted by John Leland, a prominent Baptist minister, in the halls of the House of Representatives. Throughout his presidency, Jefferson attended similar services, which were often held in the north wing of the Capitol. From 1807 to 1857, church services were held in a variety of government buildings where Congress, the Supreme Court, the War Office, and the Treasury were headquartered.

Obviously, neither Jefferson nor any other officials in the early Republic understood separation between church and state to mean that the Federal government was precluded from recognizing the necessity of public worship or from permitting active support of opportunities for such worship. Indeed, they plainly recognized that the duty of civil government was to encourage public professions of faith. Perhaps this is why John Jay, the first chief justice of the Supreme Court, specifically authorized the opening of jury sessions over which he presided with voluntary prayer led by local clergy of the Christian faith.

A Requirement for Civil Society

Many believe that James Madison, as chief architect of the Constitution and the Bill of Rights, led the fight to keep religion out of politics. In truth, he was more interested in protecting religion from politics. In 1785, two years before the Constitutional Convention, he wrote a Memorial and Remonstrance opposing a Virginia bill to establish a provision for teachers of the Christian religion. He stated that man's first duty is to God, and that "religion, or the duty which we owe to our Creator, and the manner of discharging it" was a right and a duty, "precedent both in order of time and degree of obligation, to the claims of a civil society. Before any man can be considered as a member of civil society, he must be considered as a subject of the Governor of the Universe."

Madison championed the First Amendment's Establishment Clause with one overriding purpose—to keep one sect from gaining an advantage over another through political patronage. This is a far cry from denying public worship or the public acknowledgment of God. Madison also made sure that the Establishment Clause was followed by the "Free Exercise Clause," so that the First Amendment would read, in relevant part, "Congress shall make no law respecting an establishment of religion, *or prohibiting the free exercise thereof.* . . ." (Emphasis added.)

Both Jefferson and Madison would have agreed with Supreme Court Justice Joseph Story's definitive Commentaries on the Constitution of the United States (1833), in which he posed the question of whether any free government could endure if it failed to provide for public worship. They would have concluded, as did Story, that it could not. He explained that "The promulgation of the great doctrines of religion, the being, and attributes, and providence of one Almighty God; the responsibility to him for all our actions, founded on moral freedom and accountability; a future state of rewards and punishments; the cultivation of all the personal, social, and benevolent virtues; these never can be a matter of indifference in any well ordered community. It is, indeed, difficult to conceive, how any civilized society can well exist without them.". . .

Historical Precedents

Every president of the U.S. (with only one possible exception) has been administered the oath of office with his hand on the Bible, ending with the words "so help me God." The Supreme Court begins every proceeding with the ringing proclamation, "God save the United States and this Honorable Court."

Throughout our history, the executive and legislative branches have decreed national days of fasting and prayer. Public offices and public schools close in observance of religious holidays. U.S. currency bears our national motto, "In God We Trust."

Also by law, the Pledge of Allegiance to the Flag affirms that we are "one nation under God." Congress would not even allow a comma to be placed after the word "nation" in order to reflect the basic idea that ours is a "nation founded on a belief in God."

All Containers Leak

No true wall of separation is possible. Religion and the state, the two great sources of control all through human history, will never be fully separate from each other. Each will always shade into the other's sphere. Schoolchildren learn this truth in their science classes: All containers leak. The only interesting question is how fast. In the case of religion and state, the leakage is rapid, and constant. How could matters be otherwise? Religion, by focusing the attention of the believer on the idea of transcendent truth, necessarily changes the person the believer is: which in turn changes the way the believer interacts with the world; which in turn changes political outcomes. Although there have been some clever moves in political philosophy to explain why the religious voice should not be a part of our public debates, such theories wind up describing debates from which deeply religious people are simply absent.

Besides, in a nation in which the great majority of voters describe themselves as religious, religious belief will usually be the background—even if frequently unstated—of our policy debates. A widespread religious conviction that we must aid the poor will inevitably find its way into legislation, and so the nation will create welfare programs. A widespread religious conviction that long-term help is no substitute for hard work will inevitably find its way into legislation, and so welfare will evolve into workfare.

Stephen L. Carter, *Christian Century*, October 11, 2000.

It is ludicrous and illogical to believe that it is constitutionally permissible for all three branches of the Federal government to acknowledge God openly and publicly on a regular basis, and yet, at the same time, accept the notion that the Federal government can strictly prohibit the states from doing the very same thing. Have we become so ignorant of our nation's history that we have forgotten the reason for the adoption of the Bill of Rights? It was meant to restrict the Federal government's power over the states, not to restrict them from doing what the Federal government can do.

It is no wonder that Supreme Court Justice William

Rehnquist observed in a 1985 dissenting opinion that "the wall of separation between church and state is a metaphor based upon bad history, a metaphor which has proved useless as a guide to judging. It should be frankly and explicitly abandoned.". . .

Destroying the Distinction

Since the 1960s, judicial activists have made a concerted effort to banish God from the public square. They have done this by deliberately destroying the distinction between "religion" and "religious activity." These terms may sound similar, but, in fact, they are very different. Religious activities may include many actions that would not themselves constitute religion. For example, prayer and Bible reading might be characterized as religious activities, but they do not constitute religion, and they are not limited to any specific sect or even to religious people. One may read the New Testament to gain wisdom, and school students may pray before a big exam. Neither activity was intended to be, is, or should be proscribed by the First Amendment, even if practiced in public.

However, it seems that the judicial activists are winning the war. Consider the 1997 case in DeKalb County, Ala. There, a Federal district court determined that a student's brief prayer during a high school graduation ceremony was a violation of the First Amendment because it allegedly coerced unwilling citizens to participate in religious activity. We have evidently forgotten that nothing in the Constitution guarantees that an individual won't have to see or hear things that may be disagreeable or offensive to him. We have also failed to realize that peer pressure and public opinion are not the types of coercion against which the Framers were seeking to safeguard.

No student should ever be forced by law to participate in prayer or other religious activity. However, to outlaw the public acknowledgment of God simply because another student might have to witness it is as illogical as abandoning a school mascot or motto because it might not be every student's favorite or because some might not believe in "school spirit.". . .

Liberal commentators in the media, academe, and the justice system deride the notion that restoring prayer and posting the Ten Commandments can help stem the tide of violence and bloodshed [seen in several recent school shootings]. They prefer secular solutions, especially ones that involve more Federal spending and regulation. In effect, they favor more concertina wire, metal detectors, and armed security guards instead of the simple and effective teaching of moral absolutes.

Ashamed of Faith?

Yes, teaching moral absolutes is out of the question. "We don't want to trample on the civil rights of students," they cry. "We don't want to teach that one creed or one code of conduct or one lifestyle is better than another." When will they understand that secular solutions will never solve spiritual problems?

Tragically, as in the days of the Roman Empire, we have become accustomed to "bread and circuses." With our stomachs full and our minds preoccupied with the pleasures of this world, we fail to ponder seriously the reason for the tragedies that are regularly occurring before our very eyes. We rarely contemplate the significance of the judiciary's usurpation of power and suppression of religious liberty. When and if we do, we too often are afraid to take a stand—somehow ashamed of our faith in God, afraid to hazard the notion of putting God back into the public square.

We must not wait for more violence, for a total breakdown of our schools and our communities. We must not be silent while every vestige of God is removed from our public life and every public display of faith is annihilated. The time has come to recover the valiant courage of our forefathers, who understood that faith and freedom are inseparable and that they are worth fighting for.

In the words of that great Christian and patriot, Patrick Henry, "We must fight! I repeat it, sir, we must fight! An appeal to arms and to the God of Hosts is all that is left us! . . . Why stand we here idle? What is it that the gentlemen wish? What would they have? Is life so dear, or peace so sweet, as to be purchased at the price of chains and slavery? Forbid it, Almighty God! I know not what course others may take; but as for me, give me liberty or give me death!"

"Art (and public support for the arts) must include the potential for controversy, if for no other reason than the fact that it's impossible to make everyone agree."

The Government Should Fund Art That May Be Offensive

John K. Wilson

In the following viewpoint, John K. Wilson argues that the government should continue to fund the arts, even when certain exhibits contain material that some people consider offensive or controversial. Conservatives often maintain that public funding should be withheld from museums and from artists who exhibit offensive art. But such withdrawal of funds would only amount to censorship of ideas, Wilson asserts. Conservative censors should not be allowed to judge what can and cannot be shown in museums. Wilson is the author of *The Myth of Political Correctness: The Conservative Attack on Higher Education* and *How the Left Can Win Arguments and Influence People*, from which this viewpoint is excerpted.

As you read, consider the following questions:
1. Why is censorship evil, in Wilson's opinion?
2. According to the author, what would happen to libraries if public money could not subsidize "offensive" literature?
3. In Wilson's opinion, in what way can censorship harm children?

John K. Wilson, *How the Left Can Win Arguments and Influence People*. New York: New York University Press, 2001. Copyright © 2001 by New York University Press. Reproduced by permission.

[D]uring his term], New York City Mayor Rudy Giuliani threatened to eliminate all city support for the Brooklyn Museum of Art, revoking millions of dollars unless it canceled a British exhibit called "Sensation." [This exhibit featured an image of the Virgin Mary painted with elephant dung, which some viewers considered offensive.] This was only the latest in a long line of cases in which conservative politicians punished museums, artists, and the public in order to demand that their values control public subsidies of the arts.

One of the strongest arguments for censorship is the libertarian line: no art should receive public support. It's a lovely theoretical argument, but the fact is that the public supports the arts. The question then becomes, should every institution that accepts any amount of public money be forced to capitulate to the artistic judgments of Rudy Giuliani or Jesse Helms? Nobody elected these guys to be the commanders of the thought police. As for the general issue of government funding, it seems reasonable that if we are willing to publicly fund weapons, schools, parks, highways, libraries, cops, bridges, and trillions of dollars worth of other activities, spending a minuscule part of our taxes on art strikes me as a good thing. The alternative would be for museums to sharply raise their entrance fees, effectively keeping out the poor.

Why Censorship Is Evil

If you pass a law banning public libraries from buying any books with "dirty words" in them (or punish them with budget cuts if they do), that's censorship, even if it only involves removing this "public subsidy" of dirty literature. Censorship is evil not only because it tries to punish artists or writers and the curators or librarians who pay them. Censorship is evil because it seeks to remove certain ideas and works of art from the public view.

The other main argument for censorship is the "offensiveness" line: As Giuliani puts it, "If you are a government-subsidized enterprise, then you can't do things that desecrate the most personal and deeply held views of people in society." In other words, every public institution must be devoted to the uncontroversial, the bland, the intellectual equivalent of baby food. We already have this approach to public tastes in many common areas: it's called Muzak, and it sucks. Maybe worthless crap is the best we can do in elevators, but museums are different. Nobody forces you to enter a controversial exhibit at a museum. If it offends you, leave. If you think it might offend you and the thought of being offended is so horrifying, then stay away from museums. Turn on the sit-coms, and let your brain melt on the floor if it makes you happy. But don't force everybody else to share your desire not to be offended.

Not all art that offends people is good. Some of it's downright awful. But not every book in the public library is a masterpiece, either, and that's not a reason to start a bonfire. The world of art shouldn't be a mausoleum containing only the great art of the past that is deemed acceptable to all (although even Michelangelo's *David* with his exposed penis would probably offend a lot of those congressional art critics). Art (and public support for the arts) must include the potential for controversy, if for no other reason than the fact that it's impossible to make everyone agree.

The Importance of Diversity

Progressives often get caught in the trap of defending *Piss Christ*[1] or bullwhips up butts.[2] They need to turn the National Endowment for the Arts (NEA) debate away from particular works of art and into an argument about the importance of diversity. Imagine if public libraries were prohibited from buying controversial books (as some would wish). After all, that's public money subsidizing "offensive" literature.

If an exhibit showing the Virgin Mary with elephant dung can be banned, then certainly a book showing the art in the exhibit could also be banned from the public library. And then, why not all books that insult the Virgin Mary? And since books that discuss sex and contain dirty words offend many people, toss them on the fire, too. After all, why

---

1. A photo by artist Andres Serrano of a crucifix immersed in urine   2. A reference to Robert Mapplethorpe's *Self-Portrait*, a photo of the artist bent over inserting a whip into his rectum.

should public money be used to support books and art that might offend someone?

But would you really want to see James Joyce's *Ulysses* or even lesser works of literature banned from our public libraries, or public funding withdrawn because some politician disagrees with a librarian's choice of books? That's what is at stake in the art debate.

A Tough Beauty

We are now at a point where we believe that art is confrontational by definition. When the Brooklyn Museum facetiously issued a warning that some works in the "Sensation" exhibition might cause "shock, vomiting and confusion," it, in effect, warned us that it was showing 20th-century art.

In such a mind-set, an art that engenders trust, optimism and comfort would be hopelessly retrograde. That is why so much 20th-century art seems ugly, offering a tough beauty meant to challenge our desire for peace and pleasure. The logic of the "Sensation" show is typical in this respect: We live in a culture of sensation and sensationalism, in which we thrive on a steady diet of shock and scandal and sensory stimulation, the meaning of which we do not examine. Wars, the clash of cultures and cataclysmic disasters are the standard fare of the evening news, watched at the dinner table with no apparent digestive strain. But when artists portray these same phenomena, some people are outraged, and rather than thinking about the problems art poses, they attack it for posing them indigestably. Artists might be excused for a little self-righteous glee at this response.

Wendy Steiner, *Los Angeles Times*, October 10, 1999.

Museums and art galleries display an enormous range of art, and public funding is supposed to help these institutions thrive, not to impose Rudy Giuliani's or Jesse Helms's idea of art on the rest of us. Who wants to see paintings of tobacco fields on black velvet?

Of course, no one wants a proliferation of bad art. But if a museum exhibited bad art, nobody would go to see it, and since museums can't rely on public money alone, a museum of bad art would quickly be in trouble. The censors, however, don't want to let the people or the art experts make their judgments; the censors want to tell the rest of us what we can or can't see in our public museums. Conservatives who don't like to be challenged are welcome to open "The Boring Museum for Bland Art That Offends No One" (a title that actually describes quite a few publicly subsidized museums). Far from being obsessed with the cutting edge, agencies such as the NEA and the National Endowment for the Humanities adhere to a conservative line that usually discourages innovation.

What Really Hurts Kids

One of the favorite rhetorical tricks of the right is to argue for protection of "the children." Progressives shouldn't evade this argument but counter it head on: it's censorship, not freedom of speech, that hurts our kids and corrupts their minds. The idea that a museum exhibit including dung on the Virgin Mary will turn children into serial killers seems a bit of a stretch. Children see violent acts regularly on TV, cable, and movies; they play video games full of bloody attacks; and they may even see news programs and media coverage about real-life violence, so the negative effects of going to an art museum seem a bit exaggerated in comparison. This doesn't mean we should ban Road Runner cartoons, but it does suggest that the hysteria about "offensive" art and its imagined harm to children must be kept in the proper perspective.

Worst of all, the censors like Giuliani can't see how censorship damages children's minds. When opportunistic politicians try to censor freedom of speech, children learn a powerful lesson: you shouldn't argue with opposing ideas but instead try to eliminate enemy values from public consideration. The lesson taught by Giuliani to our kids is that threats and political intimidation are the proper techniques for winning artistic debates, an idea that is far more dangerous to American values than the worst painting or sculpture imaginable.

| "Why are we being forced to subsidize willful, offensive banality?"

The Government Should Not Fund Offensive Art

Charles Krauthammer

Public funds should not be used to subsidize shocking and offensive art, contends syndicated columnist Charles Krauthammer in the following viewpoint. It is wrong to force taxpayers to support art that insults most people's sensibilities, he maintains. Moreover, those opposed to funding offensive art are not arguing for censorship. No one is demanding that vulgar art be banned or destoyed—the contention is that artists should not be entitled to government funding if they display offensive material.

As you read, consider the following questions:

1. What are some of the images included in the "Sensation" exhibition, according to Krauthammer?
2. In the author's opinion, in what way have the avant-garde been engaging in "cultural blackmail"?
3. How has the role of the artist changed in the last century and a half, in Krauthammer's view?

Charles Krauthammer, "The Mayor, the Museum, and the Madonna," *Weekly Standard*, vol. 5, October 11, 1999, pp. 14–15. Copyright © 1999 by Charles Krauthammer. Reproduced by permission.

Culture wars, chapter 36. The Brooklyn Museum of Art readies an exhibition of high decadence called "Sensation." [This exhibition included an image of the Virgin Mary painted with elephant dung, which some viewers considered offensive.] The mayor of New York threatens to close down the museum if the exhibit is not canceled. The mayor is pilloried by the usual suspects—a consortium of New York museums, the American Civil Liberties Union (ACLU), the high-brow press—for philistinism and/or First Amendment abuse.

The exhibit itself is nothing very special, just the usual *fin-de-siècle* [end of the century] celebration of the blasphemous, the criminal, and the decadent. The item that caught Rudy Giuliani's attention is a portrait of the Virgin Mary adorned with elephant dung and floating bits of female pornography. The one that caught my attention is the giant portrait of a child molester and murderer—made to look as if composed of tiny children's handprints.

The culture-guardians scream "censorship." The mayor makes the quite obvious point that these artists can do anything the hell they want, but they have no entitlement to have their work exhibited in a museum subsidized by the taxpayers of New York City to the tune of $7 million a year.

Cultural Blackmail

It is an old story. Art whose very purpose, *épater les bourgeois* ["to shock the bourgeois"], is at the same time demanding the bourgeois's subsidy. Of course, if the avant garde had any self-respect, it would shock the bourgeoisie on its own dime.

But how silly: Self-respect is a hopelessly bourgeois value. The avant garde lives by a code of fearless audacity and uncompromising authenticity. And endless financial support.

The art world has sustained this cultural blackmail by counting on the status anxiety of the middle class. They are afraid to ask the emperor's-new-clothes question—Why are we being forced to subsidize willful, offensive banality?—for fear of being considered terminally unsophisticated.

This cultural blackmail has gone on for decades, with the artist loudly blaspheming everything his patrons hold dear—while suckling at their teats. Every once in a while, however, someone refuses to play the game. This time it is Giuliani.

And sure enough, he has been charged with philistinism, or as the *New York Times* editorial put it, with making "the city look ridiculous."

"The mayor's rationale," says the *Times* with unintended hilarity, "derives from the fact that the city owns the Brooklyn Museum of Art and provides nearly a third of its operating budget."

Stayskal. © 1997 by *Tampa Tribune*. Reprinted by permission of Tribune Media Services.

Rationale? It is self-evident: You own an institution—whether you are an individual, a corporation, or a city with duly elected authorities acting on its behalf—you regulate its activity. This is no "rationale." It is a slam-dunk, argument-ending, QED clincher.

Not a Question of Censorship

Let's be plain. No one is preventing these art works from being made or displayed. The only question is whether artists have a claim on the taxpayer's dollar in displaying it.

The answer is open and shut: no. It is a question not of censorship but of sensibility. Can there ever be a limit to the tolerance and generosity of the paying public? Of course.

Does this particular exhibit forfeit whatever claim art has to public support—and the legitimacy and honor conferred upon it by the stamp of the city-owned Brooklyn Museum?

The Virgin Mary painting alone would merit an answer of yes. Add the child molester painting, the 3-D acrylic women with erect penises for noses, "Spaceshit," and "A Thousand Years" ("Steel, glass, flies, maggots, MDF, insect-o-cutor, cow's head, sugar, water, $213 \times 427 \times 213$ centimeters"), and you get a fuller picture: an artistic sensibility that is a peculiar combination of the creepy and the banal.

Of course everyone loves to play victim, the status of victim being, as Anthony Daniels put it in the *New Criterion*, "the personal equivalent of most favored nation." But the idea that art of this type is under assault or starved for funds is quite ridiculous. Art of this type is now the norm. It is everywhere. Galleries, museums, private collections are filled with it.

It is classical representational art that is starved for funds. Try finding a school in your town that teaches classical drawing or painting. As James Cooper noted some years ago in the *American Arts Quarterly*, "A modest grant to a small art academy was recently denied by the National Endowment for the Arts because, the terse NEA memo explained, 'teaching students to draw the human figure is revisionist and stifles creativity.'"

Add some dung, though, and you've got yourself a show.

The Changing Role of the Artist

The role of the artist has changed radically in the last century and a half. It was once the function of the artist to represent beauty and transcendence and possibly introduce it into the life of the beholder. With the advent of photography and film, the perfect media for both representation and narration, art has fought its dread of obsolescence by seeking some other role.

Today the function of the artist is to be an emissary to the aberrant: to live at the cultural and social extremes, to go over into the decadent and even criminal, to scout forbidden emotional and psychic territory—and bring back artifacts of that "edgy" experience to a bourgeoisie too cozy and cowardly to make the trip itself.

This has been going on for decades. It must be said, however, that at the beginning of the transformation there was an expectation that the artist would bring skill and a sense of craft to his work. Whether their conceit was dandyism, criminality, or sexual adventurism (free love, homosexuality, and the other once shocking taboos of yesterday), artists of the early modern period still felt a need to render their recreation of shock with style and technique.

Having reached a time, however, when technique itself is considered revisionist, anticreative, and, of course, bourgeois, all we are left with is the raw stinking shock. On display, right now, at the Brooklyn Museum of Art.

It is important to note that the artists and promoters who provoked the great Brooklyn contretemps are not feigning their surprise at Giuliani's counterattack. They genuinely feel entitled to their subsidy. They genuinely feel they perform a unique and priceless service, introducing vicarious extremism into the utterly compromised lives of their bourgeois patrons.

Ah, but every once in a while a burgher arises and says to the artist: No need to report back from the edge. You can stay where you are. We'll have our afternoon tea without acid, thank you.

And then the fun begins.

Periodical Bibliography

The following articles have been selected to supplement the diverse views presented in this chapter.

Taylor Caldwell — "Big Brother or Big Mommy?" *New American*, June 3, 2002.

Stephen Carter — "Beyond Neutrality," *Christian Century*, October 11, 2000.

Amitai Etzioni — "Pluralism Within Unity," *American Outlook*, Summer 1999.

Francis Fukuyama — "How to Re-Moralize America," *Wilson Quarterly*, Summer 1999.

Roger Kimball — "Art Isn't Exempt from Moral Criticism," *Wall Street Journal*, September 24, 1999.

Craig McGrath — "Think Globally, Tank Locally," *Progressive Populist*, October 1998.

Corinne McLaughlin — "Changing the World," *Tikkun*, November/December 1998.

Robert D. Novak — "The Expulsion of God," *American Legion Magazine*, May 2000.

Jeremy Patrick — "Ceremonial Deisms," *Humanist*, January/February 2002.

David Pendleton — "Good Laws and the Good Society," *America*, February 21, 1998.

John Howard Price — "One Nation, Under God," *Insight*, December 17, 2001.

Robert Royal — "Rebuild America's Morals: We Will Not Be Able to Address Questions of Justice and Security Unless We Revitalize the Practice of Public Virtue," *World & I*, January 2001.

Christopher Shea — "Among the Philistines," *American Prospect*, March 13, 2000.

Wendy Steiner — "Art in 20th Century Has Always Been 'Shock of the New,'" *Los Angeles Times*, October 10, 1999.

For Further Discussion

Chapter 1

1. Paul M. Weyrich contends that conservatives should "drop out" of American culture and find nonpolitical ways to maintain traditional values. People for the American Way and Jim Whittle maintain that right-wing activists, including Weyrich himself, never had any plans to abandon the political sphere. What do you think Weyrich's intention was when he declared that conservatives had lost the culture wars in 1999? Use evidence from the text to support your answer.

2. Stanley Kurtz argues that the culture wars reflect ongoing divisions in public opinion over controversial cultural issues, and that wide shifts in values might occur within one individual at different times in his or her life. Conversely, Christian Smith and his colleagues argue that the majority of Americans are not interested in culture wars issues. Evaluate each of these authors' viewpoints, then formulate your own argument describing the nature of America's culture wars.

3. Paul H. Ray and Sherry Ruth Anderson maintain that a new counterculture, the "cultural creatives," could find ways to move America beyond the culture wars by integrating both traditional and modern values. Do you believe that such a cultural synthesis is possible? Why or why not?

Chapter 2

1. James Harmon McElroy and David Whitman present differing views on the state of America's moral health. On what points do they agree? On what points do they disagree?

2. Jennifer A. Gritt maintains that the producers of popular culture are intentionally trying to undermine America's traditional values. Jeanne McDowell and Andrea Sachs contend that today's popular culture actually reflects Americans' love of home and community. What evidence do these authors present to support their conclusions? Whose use of evidence is more persuasive? Why?

3. John Attarian argues that the politically correct "sensitivity police" threaten individual liberty by punishing people who express opinions that allegedly offend women and minorities. How do you think Michael Bronski would respond to Attarian's argument? Explain your answer.

Chapter 3

1. Richard Parker contends that religious progressives benefit American culture by participating in struggles for economic and social justice. John Bolt maintains that religious conservatives are actually more tolerant than liberals and offer the nation its greatest hope for preserving genuine liberty. How do the supporting arguments of these two authors reflect differing ideas on the role of Judeo-Christian principles in American politics? Whose argument do you find more compelling?

2. Robert F. Morse and Tim LaHaye strongly disagree about the effects of secular humanism on society. Morse is the vice president of a Florida humanist organization; LaHaye is a conservative Christian educator and author. In what way does knowing their backgrounds influence your assessment of their arguments? Explain your answer.

3. The editors of *Rethinking Schools* define multiculturalism as a value system that opposes injustice and cultivates respect for people's various ethnic and cultural backgrounds. Bradford P. Wilson argues that multiculturalism is divisive because it focuses on alleged cultural differences rather than on unifying values and principles. In your opinion, which author's definition of multiculturalism is more accurate? Use evidence from the viewpoints to support your answer.

Chapter 4

1. Gregory Maturi contends that reasoned public debate among people of different opinions provides a means by which morality can shape law. Charles Colson argues that if Americans really want to solve their social problems, they must first embrace a common moral code—otherwise laws will be ineffective. Which perspective do you find more convincing, and why? Does the U.S. government currently prohibit certain behaviors solely on the basis of morality? List the examples cited in the viewpoints, or any others you can think of.

2. Edd Doerr wrote his viewpoint before the summer of 2002, when the U.S. Supreme Court approved the parental use of state taxes to send children to religious schools. Do you agree with Doerr that such a development constitutes a dangerous "crumbling" of the wall that separates church and state? Or do you agree with Roy S. Moore that the doctrine of church-state separation has too often been used to prevent the public acknowledgment of religion? Defend your answer with evidence from the viewpoints.

Organizations to Contact

The editors have compiled the following list of organizations concerned with the issues debated in this book. The descriptions are derived from materials provided by the organizations. All have publications or information available for interested readers. The list was compiled on the date of publication of the present volume; the information provided here may change. Be aware that many organizations take several weeks or longer to respond to inquiries, so allow as much time as possible.

American Center for Law and Justice (ACLJ)
PO Box 64429, Virginia Beach, VA 23467
(757) 226-2489 • fax: (757) 226-2836
e-mail: aclj@exis.net • website: www.aclj.org

The center is a public interest law firm and educational organization dedicated to promoting liberty, life, and the family. ACLJ provides legal services and support to attorneys and others who are involved in defending the religious and civil liberties of Americans. It publishes the booklets *Students' Rights and the Public Schools* and *Christian Rights in the Workplace*.

American Civil Liberties Union (ACLU)
125 Broad St., 18th Floor, New York, NY 10004
(212) 549-2585
website: www.aclu.org

The ACLU is a national organization that works to defend Americans' civil rights guaranteed in the U.S. Constitution. The ACLU publishes the quarterly newspaper *ACLU in Action* as well as the briefing papers "A History of Fighting Censorship" and "Preserving Artists' Right of Free Expression." Its website has a searchable archive of articles on religious liberty, students' rights, free speech, and other civil liberties issues.

Americans United for Separation of Church and State (AU)
518 C St. NE, Washington, DC 20002
(202) 466-3234 • fax: (202) 466-2587
e-mail: americansunited@au.org • website: www.au.org

AU works to protect the constitutional principle of church-state separation. It opposes mandatory prayer in public schools, tax dollars for parochial schools, and religious groups participating in politics. AU publishes the monthly *Church & State* magazine as well as issue papers, legislative alerts, reference materials, and books.

Center for the Study of Popular Culture
PO Box 67398, Los Angeles, CA 90067
(310) 843-3699 • fax: (310) 843-3692
e-mail: info@cspc.org • website: www.cspc.org

This educational center was started by commentators David Horowitz and Peter Collier, whose intellectual development evolved from support for the New Left in the 1960s to the forefront of today's conservatism. The center offers legal assistance and addresses many topics, including political correctness, multiculturalism, and discrimination. In 1993, the center launched a national network of lawyers called the Individual Rights Foundation to respond to the threat to First Amendment rights by college administrators and government officials. The center publishes the online *FrontPage* magazine.

Council for Secular Humanism
PO Box 664, Amherst, NY 14226-0664
(716) 636-7571 • fax: (716) 636-1733
e-mail: info@secularhumanism.org
website: www.secularhumanism.org

The council is an educational organization dedicated to fostering the growth of democracy, secular humanism, and the principles of free inquiry. It publishes the quarterly magazine *Free Inquiry*, and its website includes an online library containing such articles as "Why the Christian Right Is Wrong About Homosexuality" and "Responding to the Religious Right."

Fairness and Accuracy in Reporting (FAIR)
112 W 27th St., New York, NY 10001
(212) 633-6700 • fax: (212) 727-7668
e-mail: fair@fair.org • website: www.fair.org

FAIR is a national media watchdog group that investigates conservative bias in news coverage. Its members advocate greater diversity in the press and believe that structural reform is needed to break up the dominant media conglomerates and establish alternative, independent sources of information. *Extra!* is FAIR's bimonthly magazine of media criticism.

Family Research Council
801 G St. NW, Washington, DC 20001
(202) 393-2100 • (800) 225-4008
website: www.frc.org

The council is a conservative research, resource, and educational organization that promotes the traditional family. The council advocates religious liberty and opposes federal funding of the arts. It publishes *Culture Facts*, a weekly newsletter, and its website contains an online archive of papers and publications on religion and public life, arts and culture, education, and other issues.

Freedom from Religion Foundation, Inc.
PO Box 750, Madison, WI 53701
(608) 256-8900
e-mail: ffrf@mailbag.com • website: www.ffrf.org
The foundation works to keep state and church separate and to educate the public about the views of freethinkers, agnostics, and nontheists. Its publications include the newspaper *Freethought Today* and the books *Losing Faith in Faith: From Preacher to Atheist* and *The Born Again Skeptic's Guide to the Bible*.

The Heritage Foundation
214 Massachusetts Ave. NE, Washington, DC 20002-4999
(202) 546-4400 • fax: (202) 546-8328
e-mail: info@heritage.org • website: www.heritage.org
The foundation is a public policy research institute that advocates limited government, individual freedom, and traditional values. Its many publications include the position papers "Why America Needs Religion" and "God and Politics: Lessons from America's Past."

Interfaith Alliance
1331 H St. NW, 11th Floor, Washington, DC 20005
(202) 639-6370 • fax: (202) 639-6375
e-mail: tia@interfaithalliance.org
website: www.interfaithalliance.org
The Interfaith Alliance is a nonpartisan, clergy-led grassroots organization that advances a mainstream, faith-based political agenda. Its membership, which draws from more than fifty faith traditions, works to safeguard religious liberty, ensure civil rights, strengthen public education, and eradicate poverty. The alliance promotes religion as a healing and constructive force in public life and opposes the objectives of the religious right. It publishes the *Light*, a quarterly newsletter.

Media Research Center
325 S. Patrick St., Alexandria, VA 22314
(703) 683-9733 • (800) 672-1423 • fax: (703) 683-9736
e-mail: mrc@mediaresearch.org • website: www.mediaresearch.org
The center is a watchdog group that monitors liberal influence in the media. Its programs include a news division that analyzes liberal bias in mainstream news coverage. The center's publications

include *Media Reality Check*, a weekly report on news stories that have been distorted or ignored, and *Flash Report*, a monthly newsletter. The website also offers *CyberAlert*, a daily e-mail report on national media coverage.

National Coalition Against Censorship
275 Seventh Ave., New York, NY 10001
(212) 807-6222 • fax: (212) 807-6245
e-mail: ncac@ncac.org • website: www.ncac.org

The coalition represents more than forty national organizations that strive to end suppression of free speech and the press. It publishes a quarterly newsletter, *Censorship News*. Other publications include the brochure "25 Years: Defending Freedom of Thought, Inquiry and Expression," and the booklet (produced in collaboration with the National Educational Association) *Public Education, Democracy, Free Speech: The Ideas That Define and Unite Us.*

National Endowment for the Arts (NEA)
1100 Pennsylvania Ave. NW, Washington, DC 20506
(202) 682-5400
e-mail: webmgr@arts.endow.gov • website: www.nea.gov

The endowment is a federal government agency charged with supporting the arts in America. Through grants, leadership initiatives, and partnerships with public and private organizations, the NEA seeks to foster the excellence, diversity, and vitality of the arts and to broaden public access to them. Its publications include *Learning Through the Arts: A Guide to the National Endowment for the Arts* and *Arts Education, Creativity and Youth: Enriching Young Lives Through the Arts*, and an annual report.

People for the American Way Foundation
2000 M St. NW, Suite 400, Washington, DC 20036
(202) 467-4499 • (800) 326-7329
e-mail: pfaw@pfaw.org • website: www.pfaw.org

People for the American Way Foundation is a nonprofit, nonpartisan organization that opposes the political agenda of the religious right. Through public education, lobbying, and legal advocacy, the foundation defends free expression in the arts, works for equal rights for gays and lesbians, and supports public schools. The foundation's website includes Right Wing Watch, an online library of information about right-wing organizations, and the Progressive Network, a database with links to progressive organizations across the country.

Bibliography of Books

Maurianne Adams et al., eds. — *Readings for Diversity and Social Justice: An Anthology on Racism, Sexism, Anti-Semitism, Heterosexism, Classism, and Ableism.* New York: Routledge, 2000.

Amy E. Ansell, ed. — *Unravelling the Right: The New Conservatism in American Thought and Politics.* Boulder, CO: Westview Press, 1998.

James A. Banks — *An Introduction to Multicultural Education.* Boston: Allyn and Bacon, 1999.

William J. Bennett — *The Broken Hearth: Reversing the Moral Collapse of the American Family.* New York: Doubleday, 2001.

Chip Berlet and Matthew N. Lyons — *Right-Wing Populism in America: Too Close for Comfort.* New York: Guildford Press, 2000.

Robert H. Bork — *Slouching Towards Gomorrah: Modern Liberalism and American Decline.* New York: HarperCollins, 1996.

David Brock — *Blinded by the Right: The Conscience of an Ex-Conservative.* New York: Crown, 2002.

Patrick J. Buchanan — *Death of the West.* New York: St. Martin's Press, 2002.

Stephen L. Carter — *God's Name in Vain: The Wrongs and Rights of Religion in Politics.* New York: Basic Books, 2000.

Joan Chittister — *In Search of Belief.* Liguori, MO: Liguori/Triumph, 1999.

Carl Coon — *Culture Wars and the Global Village: A Diplomat's Perspective.* Amherst, NY: Prometheus, 2000.

Ronald W. Dworkin — *The Rise of the Imperial Self: America's Culture Wars in Augustinian Perspective.* Lanham, MD: Rowman & Littlefield, 2002.

Don Feder — *Who's Afraid of the Religious Right?* Ottawa, IL: Jameson Books, 1998.

Richard Feldstein — *Political Correctness: A Response from the Cultural Left.* Minneapolis: University of Minnesota Press, 1997.

Marjorie Garber — *Symptoms of Culture.* New York: Routledge, 1998.

Nathan Glazer — *We Are All Multiculturalists Now.* Cambridge, MA: Harvard University Press, 1997.

David Horowitz — *The Politics of Bad Faith: The Radical Assault on America's Future.* New York: Free Press, 1998.

James Davison Hunter   *Culture Wars: The Struggle to Control the Family, Art, Education, Law and Politics in America.* New York: Basic Books, 2000.

Robin D. Kelley   *Yo' Mama's Disfunktional: Fighting the Culture Wars in Urban America.* Boston: Beacon Press, 1998.

Roger Kimball   *The Long March: How the Cultural Revolution of the 1960s Changed America.* San Francisco: Encounter Books, 2000.

Alan Charles Kors and Harvey Silvergate   *The Shadow University: The Betrayal of Liberty on America's Campuses.* New York: Free Press, 2000.

Hilton Kramer and Roger Kimball   *The Betrayal of Liberalism: How the Disciples of Freedom and Equality Helped Foster the Illiberal Politics of Coercion and Control.* Chicago: Ivan R. Dee, 1999.

Peter Kreeft   *How to Win the Culture War: A Christian Battle Plan for a Society in Crisis.* Downers Grove, IL: InterVarsity, 2002.

Paul Kurtz   *Humanist Manifesto 2000: A Call for a New Planetary Humanism.* Amherst, NY: Prometheus, 2000.

John Leonard   *Smoke and Mirrors: Violence, Television, and Other American Cultures.* New York: New Press, 1997.

Michael Lerner   *Spirit Matters.* Charlottesville, VA: Hampton Roads, 2000.

Donald MacEdo and Lilia I. Bartolome   *Dancing with Bigotry: Beyond the Politics of Tolerance.* New York: St. Martin's Press, 2001.

Andrew M. Manis and Lewis V. Baldwin   *Southern Civil Religions in Conflict: Civil Rights and the Culture Wars.* Macon, GA: Mercer University Press, 2002.

William Martin   *With God on Our Side: The Rise of the Religious Right in America.* New York: Broadway Books, 1996.

Michael Moore   *Stupid White Men.* New York: ReganBooks, 2002.

Nancy Novosad   *Promise Keepers: Playing God.* Amherst, NY: Prometheus, 1999.

Paul H. Ray and Sherry Ruth Anderson   *The Cultural Creatives: How 50 Million People Are Changing the World.* New York: Harmony Books, 2000.

Alvin J. Schmidt   *The Menace of Multiculturalism.* Westport, CT: Greenwood, 1997.

Elaine B. Sharp, ed.   *Culture Wars and Local Politics.* Lawrence: University Press of Kansas, 1999.

Robert Shogan   *War Without End: Cultural Conflict and the Struggle for America's Political Future.* Boulder, CO: Westview Press, 2002.

Christian Smith   *Christian America?: What Evangelicals Really Want.* Berkeley: University of California Press, 2000.

Jean Stefanic and Richard Delgado   *No Mercy: How Conservative Think Tanks and Foundations Changed America's Social Agenda.* Philadelphia: Temple University Press, 1996.

Daniel A. Stout and Judith M. Buddenbaum, eds.   *Religion and Popular Culture: Studies on the Interaction of Worldviews.* Ames: Iowa State University Press, 2001.

Cal Thomas and Ed Dobson   *Blinded by Might: Can the Religious Right Save America?* Grand Rapids, MI: Zondervan, 1999.

Larry Tomlinson, Earnest N. Bracey, and Albert Cameron   *American Politics and Culture War: An Interactive Look at the Future.* Dubuque, IA: Kendall Hunt, 2002.

Brian Wallis, Marianne Weems, and Philip Yenawine, eds.   *Art Matters: How the Culture Wars Changed America.* New York: New York University Press, 1999.

Bradley C.S. Watson, ed.   *Courts and the Culture Wars.* Lanham, MD: Lexington Books, 2002.

David Whitman   *The Optimism Gap: The I'm O.K., They're Not Syndrome and the Myth of American Decline.* New York: Walker Publishing, 1998.

Rhys. H. Williams, ed.   *Cultural Wars in American Politics: Critical Reviews of a Popular Myth.* New York: Aldine de Gruyter, 1997.

John K. Wilson   *How the Left Can Win Arguments and Influence People: A Tactical Manual for Pragmatic Progressives.* New York: New York University Press, 2001.

Alan Wolfe   *Moral Freedom: The Impossible Idea That Defines the Way We Live Now.* New York: W.W. Norton, 2001.

Alan Wolfe   *One Nation, After All: What Middle-Class Americans Really Think About God, Country, Family, Racism, Welfare, Immigration, Homosexuality, the Right, the Left, and Each Other.* New York: Viking, 1998.

Jonathan Zimmerman   *Whose America?: Culture Wars in the Public Schools.* Cambridge, MA: Harvard University Press, 2002.

Index